Measuring Twice, Cutting Once

Measuring Twice, Cutting Once

Theological Reflections

JEROME C. CRICHTON

Foreword by Keith A. Burton

WIPF & STOCK · Eugene, Oregon

MEASURING TWICE, CUTTING ONCE
Theological Reflections

Copyright © 2025 Jerome C. Crichton. All rights reserved. Except for brief quotations in critical publications or reviews, no part of this book may be reproduced in any manner without prior written permission from the publisher. Write: Permissions, Wipf and Stock Publishers, 199 W. 8th Ave., Suite 3, Eugene, OR 97401.

Wipf & Stock
An Imprint of Wipf and Stock Publishers
199 W. 8th Ave., Suite 3
Eugene, OR 97401

www.wipfandstock.com

PAPERBACK ISBN: 979-8-3852-6276-2
HARDCOVER ISBN: 979-8-3852-6277-9
EBOOK ISBN: 979-8-3852-6278-6

12/16/25

Unless otherwise noted, all Scripture quotations are taken from the (NASB®) New American Standard Bible® Copyright © 1960, 1971, 1977, 1995, 2020 by The Lockman Foundation. Used by permission. All Rights reserved. lockman.org

Scripture quotations marked CSB are from The Christian Standard Bible. Copyright © 2017 by Holman Bible Publishers. Used by permission. Christian Standard Bible®, and CSB® are federally registered trademarks of Holman Bible Publishers, all rights reserved.

Scripture quotations marked NIV are from The Holy Bible, New International Version®, NIV®. Copyright © 1973, 1978, 1984, 2011 by Biblica, Inc. Used with permission of Zondervan. All rights reserved worldwide. www.zondervan.com

Scripture quotations marked ESV are from the ESV® Bible (The Holy Bible, English Standard Version®), © 2001 by Crossway, a publishing ministry of Good News Publishers. ESV Text Edition: 2025. The ESV text may not be quoted in any publication made available to the public by a Creative Commons license. The ESV may not be translated in whole or in part into any other language. Used by permission. All rights reserved.

Scripture quotations marked CJB are from the Complete Jewish Bible by David H. Stern. Copyright © 1998. All rights reserved. Used by permission of Messianic Jewish Publishers, 6120 Day Long Lane, Clarksville, MD 21029. www.messianicjewish.net.

This volume is dedicated to all those who were and have been blackballed for simply doing the art and science of theology. It is for those whose hopes and dreams have been crushed and who have found themselves ostracized and isolated because they dared to think critically in contexts that mouthed the concept of progressive revelation but didn't grasp how their own "faith" traditions have gotten to where they are or how much further they have to go.

Some a God would dare defend
To violence who is prone
Whose vengeance on an evil world
His love by wrath atones

Ordained to bear the sword they stand
As sentries by the gate
Emboldened in their zeal, assured
Their judgment He awaits

Arrayed in robes of black and white
Duty-bound in tone
An echo of their holy minds
The violence is their own

—Jerome C. Crichton

Contents

Foreword by Keith A. Burton | ix

Preface | xi

Acknowledgments | xix

Introduction | xxi

1. Redemptive Immunization Theodicy: Evil, Knowledge, and Divine Transformation | 1
2. The Social Construction of Reality: The Second Gift at Creation | 7
3. Sin: A Theological Framework | 14
4. The Radical Nature of God's Love | 19
5. Divine Love vs. Human, Socially Constructed Love | 25
6. Rereading Divorce from the Big Picture: A Theological Reappraisal of Covenant, Judgment, and Grace | 30
7. The Ineradicable Holiness of the Seventh-Day Sabbath: Holiness as Set Apart and Purposeful | 38
8. Is the Bible the Word of God? | 43
9. A Theology and Philosophy of the Soul: A Conditionalist Perspective | 53
10. A Biblical and Theological Critique of the Arbitrary Use of the Term "Remnant" | 62

CONTENTS

11 The *Ekklesia* vs. the Institutional Church: Visibility, Identity, and Divine Recognition | 71

12 The Divine Image, Complementarity, and Women in Ministry | 84

13 The Spiritual Gifts Fallacy: A Contextual and Lexical Reconsideration of 1 Corinthians 12 | 96

14 John 17:4–5: Eternity and Entropy | 104

15 The Hiddenness of God | 112

16 Biblical and Theological Analysis of Tithing | 126

17 A Biblical Theology Undercutting Assumptions about the "Former and Latter Rain" in Joel and Acts | 131

18 The Permanence of the Clean/Unclean Distinction: A Covenantal and Moral Framework for Understanding Covenantal Violations as Spiritual Rebellion | 136

19 Kings, Queens, and the Gang That Won: A Deconstruction of Romans 13 and Divine Authority | 142

20 Institutional Authority and the Queer Identified | 148

Postscript: Theology as Art and Science—The Divine Invitation to Progressive Revelation | 155

About the Author | 159

Bibliography | 161

General Index | 173

Scripture Index | 177

Foreword

As a do-it-yourselfer who infrequently dabbles in carpentry projects, I am still learning to trust the wisdom in the carpenter's proverb "Measure twice, cut once." Having reprimanded myself several times after costly do-overs, I am gradually learning that the proverb is more than a call to craftsmanship, but an invitation to exercise patience and care. In his brilliant adaptation of this sage advice, Dr. Jerome Crichton applies the proverb to hermeneutics, which he defines as both craft and art. In his positively provocative coverage of a variety of themes, he reminds us that theology, like carpentry, deals with issues too precious to handle carelessly.

Measuring Twice, Cutting Once challenges in ways that serious hermeneutics should. Not content with packaged, pet propaganda that passes as serious theology, the study invites us to take a step back before engaging a theological theme. If we are to move closer toward truth, we must be willing to pause before we speak, to reflect before we teach, and to weigh our convictions before we build our doctrines into stone. In a time when many are tempted to mistake confidence for clarity, Dr. Crichton offers a refreshing model of measured faith—one that is honest about questions, courageous in conviction, and submissive before God's word.

As readers take the measured trek through these pages, they will notice a syncopated sensitivity as each subject melds together in a jazz harmony in a way that allows the reader to appreciate why they occupy the same space. Each chapter embodies a gentle rhythm of reflection and reexamination, as it wrestles with truth in a complex dialogue with

FOREWORD

Protestant Scripture, with church tradition, with reason, and with experience. As Dr. Crichton develops his succinct arguments, the Wesleyan Quadrilateral is slightly influenced by a Hegelian quest to quell the dialectic in search of a more accurate synthesis. For Dr. Crichton, this is not a mere game of intellectual jousting but aims toward spiritual honesty. In his pastoral fashion, he teaches us that faith does not fear tension; rather, it uses tension as the Spirit's workshop, a place where rough edges are shaped into understanding.

Even as Dr. Crichton selects the data that will serve as measuring instruments, he recognizes how easily our own minds can mislead us. He challenges the confirmation bias that makes us hear only what we want to hear and the cognitive dissonance that often tempts us to silence the Spirit's unsettling voice. By naming these inner struggles, he reminds us that honest hermeneutics demands the discipline of self-examination. We are called not to a blind certainty, but to a trustful awareness as we allow the Spirit to test the measurements of our hearts.

Foundational to this study is Dr. Crichton's belief in progressive revelation. For him, God's truth continues to unfold, not because God changes, but because our insights deepen. The theologian who measures twice does not discard the voluminous discoveries of those who labored in the past. Instead, she honors them by remeasuring the cut, ensuring that the structure of belief still fits the contours of God's living word. Even as she does this, there is a humble awareness that further measurement may be necessary in the future.

While covering serious—and sometimes controversial—theological themes, this book is not only for scholars. It is for every believer who has ever thought about why they believe what they believe, and asked, "Did I measure that rightly?" Dr. Crichton's reflections give us permission to ask again, to measure again, and to let grace guide our next cut.

As you read, you will sense both the scholar and the pastor, the thinker and the shepherd. The result is theology with a heartbeat—insights delivered with tenderness, courage tempered by compassion. These pages will challenge you to think deeply, love boldly, and follow faithfully the One whose own hands still bear the marks of perfect craftsmanship.

KEITH A. BURTON, PHD
AdventHealth University

Preface

THIS VOLUME IS A direct product of my tenure at Every Word Ministries in the East Bay of San Francisco, California. I cannot express sufficiently the beauty of the spirit that has bound us together for nearly three decades. Although other influences have contributed to this project, the primary inspiration leading to its completion has been the gift of the Spirit, bestowed week after week as we endeavored to engage and embrace every word. Again, thank you to my Every Word Ministries family; this volume represents, in part, your investment in the gospel ministry.

Yet, even as this work draws from such enriching communal roots, it also confronts the broader challenges facing theological discourse in many denominations today.

Many mainline denominations, like my own, suffer from theological fragility. They spend a lot of time and energy building walls and placing sentries around them, along with career gatekeepers who opportunistically seek ways to advance in the ranks—sometimes at any cost, and most times eviscerating their consciences in order to gain the affirmation of the institutional movers and shakers and to protect the interests of the institution.

Often, these gatekeepers have confused their career aspirations with the call to gospel ministry—a confusion consequent to being blinded by the fantasy of personal ambition. Their desire to be somebody expresses itself as lower spiritual sensibilities, which inevitably inspire their justification for weeding out those who may exercise unusual scrutiny or be more critically inclined.

PREFACE

This is nothing new. Note Jesus' caution to his disciples in the first century:

> "These things I have spoken to you so that you will not be led into sin. They will ban you from the synagogue, yet an hour is coming for everyone who kills you to think that he is offering a service to God. These things they will do because they have not known the Father nor Me. But these things I have spoken to you, so that when their hour comes, you may remember that I told you of them. However, I did not say these things to you at the beginning, because I was with you." (John 16:1–4)

Few of the gatekeepers in the first century would have seen themselves as not knowing the Father; and it is no less true today. It may be that they have a misplaced fidelity. They may have mistakenly given to their employer the fidelity due to God alone because they see their employer as being synonymous with God or as an extension of God. There may be other less obvious reasons, but here's the thing:

> My conscience is captive to the Word of God. I cannot and will not recant anything, for to go against conscience is neither right nor safe.[1]

This volume confidently asserts that revelation is progressive. God unfolds his word to us over time, so theological thinking and exploration should never be the slave of the career types, who are akin to preservative in a loaf of bread. With or without them, God has provided the means by which our vision through a dark glass will become clearer, as long as we do not fear to challenge previous assumptions, knowing that ours will also be challenged should time last. My hope is that—should time last—I will become a casualty of this book title; it is the privilege of writing theology. But more than that, it is the Spirit's reminder that he is committed to the work that councils, boards, synods, and committees can never accomplish.

Many institutions insist that their adherents live by bread alone, as if the word that proceeds out of the mouth of God is not fresh each day. Their stranglehold on their interpretations betrays an unwillingness to yield to the Spirit, who is commissioned to guide us "into all the truth" (John 16:13), not by some mystical sleight of hand but through

---

1. Martin Luther, quoted in Bainton, *Here I Stand*, 185.

the prayerful efforts of those who give themselves to prayer and study, just as in ages past.

Gone ought to be the days when an individual's career or even their life is threatened because they have the nerve to challenge sacred institutional cows. If those cows can stand the scrutiny they will only be strengthened, but if not, the landscape will be littered with their waste.

My hope is simply to contribute to the progress of better understanding the Scriptures as we think about them and reflect on them, in the hope of contributing to the liberation for which Christ died.

MEASURE TWICE, CUT ONCE: ON THE COST OF THEOLOGICAL IMPULSES

There's a carpenter's proverb whispered in workshops and woodshops across the world: "Measure twice, cut once." It's a phrase born out of hard-earned wisdom—the kind that anticipates the permanent consequences of imprecision. A board once cut too short cannot be stretched. A hole once drilled in the wrong place cannot be undrilled. And the saw, once it's in motion, doesn't pause to ask if you've thought things through.

Theology, I've come to believe, is not so different.

Theological reflection is the sacred act of handling revealed truth. It is one part inquiry, one part humility, and one part reverence. But too often, theological work—especially when driven by ambition, tradition, or fear—treats the saw as more important than the ruler. We see something that looks true, feels urgent, or satisfies the moment, and we cut. We carve out doctrines, pronounce finalities, build institutions—and sometimes excommunicate souls—with measurements we never double-checked. The result? Wounds that linger, and sometimes entire generations that walk away from the faith not because of Christ, but because of our mismeasured certainties about him.

This book is titled *Measuring Twice, Cutting Once* for a reason. It is a call to theological caution and theological humility. It is not an invitation to indecision or intellectual paralysis, but to responsible inquiry, the

PREFACE

acknowledgment that theological commitments—once made—shape lives, form consciences, dictate behavior, and bear eternal consequence.

THEOLOGICAL SCARS THAT NEVER HEAL

Consider the doctrine of race-based slavery, once taught from pulpits and defended with verses wrenched out of context (e.g., Gen 9:25; Eph 6:5). Or the marginalization of women under the guise of "biblical roles," often more cultural than scriptural (cf. Gal 3:28). Or the prosperity gospel's dangerous claim that faith guarantees healing—leaving the sick ashamed and the poor spiritually bereft (cf. 2 Cor 12:7–10).

Each of these examples represents a failure to measure twice.

They are the result of theology done uncarefully—cutting before measuring, speaking before listening to the full arc of Scripture, and embracing interpretations that suit personal or cultural interests. And even when such errors are later recanted, their cuts remain deep—splitting families, severing faith, and disfiguring the *ekklesia*'s witness. To be sure, theology is not merely about avoiding mistakes. It is also about courageously committing to the truth once it is discovered. But how we arrive at that truth matters, and how soon we declare others wrong matters even more.

JESUS AND THE DOUBLE MEASUREMENT

Jesus modeled the kind of theological wisdom that our generation desperately needs. He was never rushed into judgment. He asked probing questions:

> "What is written in the Law? How does it read to you?" (Luke 10:26)

He discerned the heart beneath the issue:

> "You examine the Scriptures because you think that in them you have eternal life; and it is those very Scriptures that testify about Me." (John 5:39)

He challenged assumptions without resorting to cynicism. He measured twice—weighing truth not only by the letter but by the Spirit and purpose of God's redemptive plan. When religious leaders tried to trap him with a woman caught in adultery, Jesus didn't immediately respond with condemnation or cheap grace. He paused. He knelt. He wrote. Only then did he say,

> "He who is without sin among you, let him be the first to throw a stone at her." (John 8:7)

It was a moment of both caution and clarity—a double measurement that saved a life and taught the crowd the meaning of divine justice and mercy.

WHY WE'RE OFTEN TEMPTED TO CUT TOO SOON

There are many reasons why theologians, pastors, and even lay Christians move too quickly toward conclusions:

- *Tradition*: We inherit beliefs that are rarely questioned because "they've always been taught." But longevity does not equal infallibility.
- *Fear*: When confronted with ambiguity, we prefer the illusion of certainty, even if it's built on shaky foundations.
- *Ambition*: In academic and ecclesial circles, bold theological claims often gain more attention than nuanced ones. Controversy sells; caution rarely does.
- *Tribalism*: We want to belong. So, we mirror the views of our group and silence internal tensions for fear of exclusion.

But theology, if it is to serve truth, must resist these impulses. It must be willing to challenge itself. It must allow Scripture to surprise us, even offend us, and ultimately transform us. And that can only happen if we measure not just once, but twice.

REMEASUREMENT IS NOT HERESY

Theological growth sometimes requires rethinking old assumptions. This is not heresy—it is faithfulness. Peter had to be corrected by a rooftop vision (Acts 10) to realize that gentiles were not unclean. Paul, once zealous for the law, became the apostle of grace (Gal 1:13–16). The

PREFACE

Council of Jerusalem had to debate whether circumcision was necessary (Acts 15). These were not minor tweaks; they were paradigm shifts. And they came through reaction and reflection, not by cutting first but by measuring again in light of Christ.

To be clear, this book is not written from a posture of skepticism or theological rebellion. It is written from a place of reverence—reverence for the word of God, reverence for the cost of doctrinal error, and reverence for the humility modeled by Jesus. It is my belief that many doctrines long held as unquestionable are due for remeasurement—not because truth has changed, but because our understanding of it has often remained shallow.

CUTTING RIGHT: WHEN PRECISION IS LIBERATION

When we do finally cut—when we speak, teach, write, or preach—we must do so with clarity born of study. Measuring twice guards against both error and arrogance.

When Martin Luther nailed his ninety-five theses to the doors of the Wittenberg Castle, it was not without forethought; he had measured.[2] When the early church debated the divinity of Christ, they didn't rush; they deliberated.[3] And when the apostle Paul wrote his letters, they were not just opinion pieces; they were the result of contemplating the Scriptures and wrestling with the Spirit.

In the same way, this volume is a series of theological reflections offered with care. Each chapter wrestles with doctrines that matter deeply—evil, redemption, ecclesiology, holiness, the soul, and the Sabbath—not as a final word, but as a contribution to the greater conversation. You may find in these pages perspectives you've never considered, or challenges to assumptions you hold dear. My aim is not to provoke for provocation's sake, but to encourage careful remeasurement, always guided by the Holy Spirit and the full counsel of Scripture.

---

2. Bainton, *Here I Stand*, 144–45.
3. Pelikan, *Christian Tradition*, 172–203.

A DEDICATION TO THOSE WHO'VE PAID THE PRICE

Finally, this work is dedicated to those who were blackballed, marginalized, or misunderstood—not for departing from truth, but for daring to measure again what others had cut, perhaps prematurely. Theology, at its best, is not gatekeeping but shepherding. It invites and encourages honest questions; it decries dishonest certainties.

If you've ever been told that thinking critically is tantamount to rebellion, or your questions are a threat to the faith—you are not alone. The *ekklesia* needs your discernment. Your theological voice, tempered with humility, may be exactly what helps others measure a second time.

So, we begin—not with the threat of death, being blackballed, or being expelled but with the understanding that we are indebted to thinkers who understood their allegiance to God and saw their work not as pure science but as art and science. They exhibited the spirit of the Bereans, who were "more noble-minded than those in Thessalonica" (Acts 17:11).

Acknowledgments

My heartfelt gratitude goes out to Every Word Ministries and those past and present who have supported and continue to support our collective mission. You have helped to sustain me through thick and thin and have given impetus to this volume by allowing me to serve you going on three decades. This volume is possible because of you. Thank you! I love you!

To Dr. Keith Augustus Burton, my colleague and countryman of shared roots and educational journey; you have always been such a great inspiration toward biblical scholarship. Your love for the kingdom and its subjects is reflected in your writing, teaching, and preaching.

Introduction

THIS BOOK'S EPIGRAPH PAINTS a portrait of a dangerous piety. It describes a divine enforcer, a god of retribution whose defenders stand as sentries at the gate of orthodoxy, armed with the sword of judgment, assured of their own vindication. Their violence—theological, institutional, and sometimes even physical—is not seen as a flaw but as a feature of their fidelity. They are arrayed in the black and white of absolute certainty, and the poem's chilling conclusion reveals that the violence they wield is, ultimately, their own. It is a product of their "holy minds," a reflection of their own construction of God.

This volume is an extended theological conversation with these sentries and the god they defend.

The chapters that follow proceed from a conviction: the God revealed in Jesus Christ cannot be contained within this framework. The task of theology is to "measure twice" this dominant image of God against the full counsel of Scripture—to question whether the sentries are guarding a truth or an idol. This is not an act of rebellion, but of profound faithfulness. It is the work of ensuring that our conception of God is worthy of him and consistent with the one who said,

> "Take My yoke upon you and learn from Me, for I am gentle and humble in heart." (Matt 11:29)

Therefore, this book is organized as a journey of deconstruction and reconstruction. We begin by confronting the fundamental problems that give rise to the need for such a vengeful deity. The first section focuses on the foundations of reality, opening with a *redemptive immunization theodicy*, arguing that God permits evil not as punishment but as a paradoxical means of inoculating creation against its eternal recurrence. It then explores the *social construction of reality*, examining how we, as God's image-bearers, create frameworks of meaning that can either reveal or obscure divine truth. This section culminates in a novel framework for understanding *sin* not merely as act, but as a capricious, pervasive force that manifests physically, metaphysically, and transcendentally.

With this foundation established, the next section considers the nature of love, seeking to rebuild a vision of God from the ground up. It contrasts the radical, holy, and covenantal love of God with its human, socially constructed counterfeit. This theological groundwork then enables a courageous rereading of *divorce*, not as a pastoral exception but as a category deeply embedded in—and modeled by—God's own covenant history.

The third section looks at structures of authority, bringing this refined theology to bear on the institutions and doctrines often wielded as weapons. It argues for the *ineradicable holiness of the seventh-day sabbath* as a creation ordinance, critiques the arbitrary use of the "remnant" label, and deconstructs the modern concept of "spiritual gifts." A robust exploration of the question *Is the Bible the word of God?* clarifies its derivative authority as the God-breathed text that reliably reveals the ultimate Word, Jesus Christ. This section also includes a conditionalist perspective on the *theology of the soul* and a challenge to interpretations of Rom 13 that would divinely sanction the authority of "the gang that won."

Finally, the last section considers the boundaries of *ekklesia*, applying this entire framework to the most pressing ecclesial questions. It sharply distinguishes the organic *ekklesia* from the institutional church, arguing that the latter often usurps the role of the Spirit. This liberating distinction informs a fresh approach to *women in ministry* and a biblical critique of *tithing* as a new-covenant expectation. The volume concludes by confronting the church's treatment of *queer-identified* individuals, arguing that institutional gatekeeping based on attribution and consensus lacks the divine authority to override the Shepherd who alone knows his sheep.

Each chapter is an exercise in measuring twice. It is a call to move beyond the black-and-white robes of simplistic certainty and to embrace the complex, beautiful, and sometimes mysterious colors of a God whose thoughts are not our thoughts. This is not a work of skepticism, but of hope—a hope that a more careful measurement will lead to a more faithful cut, and that a more faithful cut will lead to a more compelling witness to the world.

The sentries may stand by the gate. This work invites you to step inside.

1

Redemptive Immunization Theodicy
Evil, Knowledge, and Divine Transformation

THE PROBLEM OF EVIL has haunted theological discourse for centuries. If God is all-powerful and all-good, why does evil exist? The redemptive immunization theodicy (RIT) offers a compelling response: God permits evil not as an end in itself, but as a means of bringing about a greater good—one in which humanity retains the knowledge of good and evil but is ultimately freed from its destructive power. Unlike traditional theodicies that either justify the suffering that results from evil as soul-making or dismiss it as an unsolvable mystery, RIT presents evil as a paradoxical instrument in God's redemptive plan. It asserts that a world in which evil is defeated is a better world than a world with the potential for evil.

The redemptive immunization theodicy is grounded in the conviction that God permitted the knowledge of good and evil to enter the human experience not as a divine accident, but as a deliberate opportunity to render evil permanently impotent. It begins with the assertion that Adam and Eve were not created in an immature state, as suggested by Irenaeus, but rather were endowed with volitional freedom, capable of obedience or disobedience. The tree of the knowledge of good and evil, placed in Eden, served as a demonstration of this freedom—a concrete manifestation of their capacity for moral agency.

The theological innovation of RIT lies in its interpretation of the knowledge of good and evil as a realm of knowledge that only God could bear without corruption. Once breached by Adam and Eve, this knowledge introduced them to a domain of moral reality where evil, as the corruption of good, could entice and destroy. Their fall was not merely a disobedient act, but a volitional, ontological rupture that exposed humanity to suffering, decay, and death—consequences not arbitrarily imposed, but inherent in the knowledge they acquired.

Yet God, in his redemptive foresight, allowed this rupture to serve a pedagogical function. In permitting evil and suffering, God ordained that humanity would ultimately be immunized against evil—not by avoidance, but by redemptive encounter. In this framework, pain and suffering are not ends in themselves, nor arbitrary punishments, but elements of a divine strategy to ensure that while evil will be known in the new creation, it will never again be desired. Evil's seductive power is starved through the experience of it and renders it impotent.

This immunization reaches its fulfillment through glorification in Christ, as detailed in John 17:20–24. Christ's wounds serve as the redemptive memory of human suffering, rendering detailed traumatic memory unnecessary in the restored order (Rev 21:3–4). Thus, the RIT asserts that divine recreation does not eliminate the knowledge of good and evil, but disarms it permanently because no one who is redeemed—by virtue of their experience and their understanding of its cost—will have an appetite for it.

SCRIPTURAL FOUNDATIONS OF RIT

The scriptural foundation of the redemptive immunization theodicy rests on several key texts that affirm both the moral freedom of humanity and the redemptive purpose of suffering.

Genesis 2:16–17 introduces the tree of the knowledge of good and evil not as a trap, but as a moral boundary meant to validate volition. Genesis 3:22 reveals that post-fall, humans acquired knowledge that made them "like God," suggesting they were privy to knowledge that was potent and dangerous.

Romans 8:18–21 frames suffering as preparatory, with creation itself waiting for redemption. This aligns with the RIT notion that suffering contributes to eternal immunity against evil. Isaiah 65:17 says, and Rev 21:4 confirms, that in the new creation, the "former things will not be remembered or come to mind," yet this does not imply amnesia but transformation, as the presence of the glorified Christ renders detailed recollection unnecessary.

John 17:20–24 is central to RIT. Jesus prays that his followers would be united with him and the Father, a metaphysical union that secures final incorruptibility—where evil is known, but never again desired.

The narrative begins in Gen 2–3, where Adam and Eve are given a single prohibition:

> "From the tree of the knowledge of good and evil you shall not eat, for on the day that you eat from it you will certainly die." (Gen 2:17)

The serpent's assertion—"you will become like God, knowing good and evil" (Gen 3:5)—was deceptively subtle and inferred that they, like God, would be able to handle knowing good and evil. Prior to their deception, they had only known good by experience; the coin had only one side. To know the other side experientially was a domain that God kept from them because they were not created to handle it. They were created with a limitation that once breached would result in death.

The resulting consequences of the breach suggest that this knowledge was not merely intellectual but experiential. They disobeyed by an act that affected their being and their knowing, gaining moral awareness at the cost of corruption. The apostle Paul later develops this theme in Rom 5, contrasting Adam's disobedience with Christ's obedience. Where Adam brought death, Christ brings life; where sin abounded, grace abounded more (Rom 5:20). This framework is crucial for RIT because it suggests that evil is not a permanent condition but a temporary state that God will ultimately subvert.

HISTORICAL PRECEDENTS: EARLY CHURCH INSIGHTS

Having established the scriptural foundations of RIT, we now explore its resonance with early church insights, which further illuminate its theological depth. While RIT breaks from Irenaeus's view of humanity as created immature, it aligns with some patristic themes. Athanasius, in *On the Incarnation*, speaks of Christ entering the corruption of the world to restore the image of God in humanity—resonating with RIT's idea of redemptive exposure.[1] Augustine, for instance, argued that evil is not a substance but a privation of good—like darkness, which exists only as the absence of light.[2] His emphasis on humanity's fall and redemption aligns with RIT's view that evil is a corruption rather than a creation of God.

Gregory of Nyssa took a different approach, envisioning salvation as *epektasis*, an eternal progression toward God. In this view, suffering is not meaningless but serves as a refining fire, preparing humanity for greater glory.[3] *The Great Catechism* envisions a teleological development of humanity into divine likeness, though RIT diverges by affirming full moral volition from creation. Augustine's *City of God* emphasizes the final inability of the redeemed to sin (*non posse peccare*), a concept compatible with RIT's notion of permanent immunity without coercion.[4] Athanasius saw Christ's incarnation as the restoration of the divine image in humanity—a theme central to RIT's claim that God redeems through suffering rather than in spite of it.[5] The wounds of Christ, often referenced in medieval devotion, are also taken up in RIT as the eschatological memory of evil—retained not in trauma, but in glorified form (cf. Rev 5:6).

CONTEMPORARY THEOLOGICAL ENGAGEMENT

Building upon these historical precedents, contemporary theologians offer further insights that align with RIT's vision of redemptive suffering. Hans Urs von Balthasar, in *Theo-Drama*, presents a vision of divine drama where suffering has narrative necessity—this aligns with RIT's pedagogical view of evil.[6] Eleonore Stump's work on suffering, particularly in *Wandering in Darkness*, affirms that redemptive suffering builds the kind of knowledge that mere instruction cannot, closely echoing RIT's theme of experiential inoculation.[7] Marilyn McCord

---

1. Athanasius, *On the Incarnation*, 55.
2. Augustine, *City of God*, trans. Bettenson, 11.9.3 (590).
3. Gregory of Nyssa, *Great Catechism*, 478.
4. Augustine, *City of God*, trans. Bettenson, 22.30.3 (1012).
5. Athanasius, *On the Incarnation*, 78.
6. Von Balthasar, *Theo-Drama*, 245.
7. Stump, *Wandering in Darkness*, 321.

Adams, in *Horrendous Evils and the Goodness of God*, emphasizes the role of divine participation in suffering—a key element in RIT's focus on the cross as interpretive center.[8] While none of these theologians explicitly articulate RIT, their works converge on its major pillars: suffering as revelatory, Christ as mediator of transformation, and the eschaton as a state of incorruptible freedom grounded in divine love.

THEOLOGICAL INTEGRATION: SIN, SALVATION, AND THE SPIRIT

With these theological convergences in view, we now integrate RIT's framework through the lenses of hamartiology, soteriology, pneumatology, and eschatology.

First, sin is not merely wrongdoing but a fractured way of being and knowing. The fall distorted human sensation and perception because neither were constructed to handle good and evil. Yet RIT insists that the knowledge of good and evil—now destructive—will one day be subjugated and subdued.

Second, salvation in Christ does more than forgive; ultimately, it immunizes. Just as exposure to a weakened virus trains the body to resist disease, Christ's incarnation, crucifixion, and resurrection assure that the knowledge of good and evil will have no power over a redeemed humanity.

Third, the Holy Spirit plays a vital role as the divine immunizing agent. Believers are transformed and sanctified through the Spirit—not by erasing the past but by integrating it into the larger framework of redemption.

Finally, eschatology completes the picture. Glorification is not amnesia; it is the full realization of what Paul describes in 1 Cor 13:12:

> For now we see in a mirror dimly, but then face to face; now I know in part, but then I will know fully just as I also have been fully known.

The scars of history remain, but they are transfigured, much like Christ's resurrected wounds (John 20:27).

---

8. Adams, *Horrendous Evils*, 154.

ORIGINAL CONTRIBUTIONS OF RIT

The redemptive immunization theodicy offers several original contributions to theodicy and systematic theology:

1. **Rejection of the Irenaean model:** RIT contends that Adam and Eve were not morally immature but fully volitional beings. The tree of the knowledge of good and evil was not a soul-building mechanism, but a means of demonstrating volition.

2. **Distinction between divine prerogative and divine pedagogy:** The knowledge of good and evil was forbidden as a divine prerogative and was not intended to be instructive; disobedience would result in corruption.

3. **Evil as pedagogical and existing prior to the creation of Adam and Eve:** RIT frames evil as a cosmic reality known to God and the angelic realm before human history. Its entrance into human experience is permitted for the purpose of eternal inoculation.

4. **Christ's wounds as redemptive memory:** RIT asserts that detailed human recollection of trauma is unnecessary in the eschaton because Christ's glorified scars function as the eternal memorial of redemptive suffering.

5. **Glorification as metaphysical transformation grounded in union with Christ:** Drawing from John 17:20–24, RIT claims that final incorruptibility arises not from moral progress alone, but from relational participation in divine life.

6. **Suffering as the agent of immunity:** Unlike traditional theodicies that justify suffering only by future compensation or soul-making, RIT proposes that suffering disarms evil by revealing its futility and ensuring its rejection.

2

The Social Construction of Reality
The Second Gift at Creation

IN GENESIS, GOD BESTOWS two profound gifts upon humanity. The first, "be fruitful and multiply," establishes the reproductive and dominion mandate (Gen 1:28). The second, subtler yet equally transformative, is the capacity to name, classify, and construct shared meaning: the social construction of reality. This divine endowment is introduced when God brings the animals to Adam "to see what he would call them" (Gen 2:19). The text notes that "whatever the man called each living creature, that was its name." This moment marks the inception of abstract reasoning, consensus formation, symbolic language, and the taxonomy of reality, all rooted in humanity's unique role as image-bearers.

This chapter explores the theological and anthropological implications of this second gift. It argues that humanity was endowed not only with biological fecundity but also with cognitive and communal creativity—an ability to frame and interpret existence in ways that mirror the divine Logos (John 1:1–3) yet require moral and spiritual calibration. Crucially, this capacity is undergirded by the interplay of faith and reason as the epistemological foundation of reality, as evidenced by Rom 1:20 and Heb 11:3, which reveal that reality is apprehended through a synergy of rational observation and faith in divine revelation. By analyzing key biblical texts, patristic insights, and modern theories of social epistemology, we demonstrate that the social construction of reality is neither neutral nor autonomous. It must be exercised under the sovereignty of God and guided by divine revelation. Without such anchoring, this gift devolves into confusion, as seen in Babel (Gen 11:1–9) and echoed in today's fragmented moral landscapes.

BIBLICAL FOUNDATIONS

The concept of humanity constructing reality is first illustrated in Gen 2:19–20, where God tasks Adam with naming the animals:

> Out of the ground the LORD God formed every beast of the field and every bird of the sky, and brought them to the man to see what he would call them; and whatever the man called a living creature, that was its name.

This act signifies not mere labeling but categorizing, interpreting, and participating in creation through rational and symbolic thought, a process grounded in the *imago Dei*.

In naming, Adam exercises a prerogative granted by God—a symbolic co-regency over creation. This mirrors God's own act of speaking creation into existence (Gen 1:3, 6, 9). The Word (Logos) functions both to bring reality into being and to sustain its order (cf. John 1:1–3; Heb 1:3). Human beings, created in the *imago Dei*, share a limited capacity to shape reality through speech, meaning, and agreement. This is reinforced in Prov 18:21: "Death and life are in the power of the tongue."

Romans 1:20 and Heb 11:3 establish the interplay of faith and reason as the epistemological foundation for apprehending reality. Romans 1:20 states,

> For since the creation of the world His invisible attributes, that is, His eternal power and divine nature, have been clearly perceived, being understood by what has been made, so that they are without excuse.

This verse affirms that reality is revelatory, accessible through rational observation of the created order, which bears intelligible signs of God's attributes. Yet, this understanding is completed by faith, which discerns the divine purpose behind the visible world, making humans epistemically accountable.

Hebrews 11:3 further clarifies,

THE SOCIAL CONSTRUCTION OF REALITY

> By faith we understand that the world has been created by the word of God so that what is seen has not been made out of things that are visible.

This text positions faith as a rational mode of knowing, enabling humans to grasp the nonmaterial origin of reality—creation ex nihilo—beyond empirical limits. Together, these verses underscore that reason and faith work in concert to perceive reality's structure and meaning, pointing to a transcendent source.

The Tower of Babel (Gen 11:1–9) illustrates the dangers of autonomous reality construction. Humanity, united in language and intent, sought to build a city and a tower to "make a name" for themselves apart from divine direction. God disrupts their plans by confusing their language, revealing that the social construction of reality is only legitimate when aligned with divine authority, apprehended through faith and reason. Autonomous construction leads to confusion and dispersion, fracturing human unity and purpose.

Isaiah 5:20 condemns those who "call evil good, and good evil," indicting corrupted social frameworks. Jesus challenges socially constructed norms: "You have heard it said . . . but I say to you" (Matt 5:21–48), revealing how divine revelation, accessed through faith, reorients human categories. The apostle Paul urges believers not to be conformed to the pattern of this world but to be "transformed by the renewing of your mind" (Rom 12:2), affirming the role of a faith-informed epistemology.

The New Testament underscores the redemptive reconstruction of reality through the mind of Christ (1 Cor 2:16). Believers are called to interpret the world through the lens of revealed truth, guided by the Holy Spirit and informed by faith and reason (John 16:13). Thus, biblical theology insists that reality is not merely perceived—it is divinely interpreted and morally accountable, with faith and reason as its epistemological anchors.

THEOLOGICAL AND PHILOSOPHICAL INSIGHTS

The social construction of reality has deep roots in theological anthropology and philosophical epistemology. Theologically, the *imago Dei* implies rationality, relationality, and the capacity to create meaning, all of which are informed by the interplay of faith and reason (Rom 1:20; Heb 11:3). As Augustine noted, ordering one's love (*ordo amoris*) is fundamental to rightly perceiving and interpreting the world. In *City of God*, he writes:

> Living a just and holy life requires one to be capable of an objective and impartial evaluation of things: to love things, that is to say, in the right order.[1]

Misordered loves distort perception, leading to false constructions of value and identity, which faith and reason, rightly aligned, correct.

Philosophically, Peter Berger and Thomas Luckmann's *The Social Construction of Reality* underscores how knowledge is produced through social interaction, habitualization, and institutionalization.[2] Their theory, while insightful, often neglects the theological necessity of grounding knowledge in divine revelation. Christian theology challenges the notion that all reality is equally valid when socially agreed upon. Scripture insists that divine revelation, apprehended through faith and reason, is the standard by which all constructs must be measured (Ps 119:105; Rom 1:20).

Abraham Kuyper argued that all spheres of life are subject to the lordship of Christ.[3] Human institutions and knowledge structures must be subordinated to the word of God, which faith and reason enable us to apprehend (Heb 11:3). Cornelius Van Til emphasized that human knowledge is derivative, finding legitimacy only when rooted in God's self-disclosure.[4] Contemporary theologians like Alister McGrath and Kevin Vanhoozer reaffirm that theology is not merely a language game but a participation in divine communication, guided by faith and reason.[5] Reality is not endlessly pliable; it is shaped by God's speech and covenantal intent. Social construction, when untethered from divine authority, becomes idolatrous—a Tower of Babel dressed in academic robes.

---

1. Augustine, *City of God*, trans. Bettenson, 15.22 (573).
2. Berger and Luckmann, *Social Construction of Reality*, 44–64.
3. Kuyper, *Lectures on Calvinism*, 79–80.
4. Van Til, *Defense of the Faith*, 43–45.
5. McGrath, *Scientific Theology*, 195–200; Vanhoozer, *Drama of Doctrine*, 265–70.

HISTORICAL THEOLOGY AND THE USE OF LANGUAGE

Throughout church history, language has been recognized as a theological and moral act. The early church fathers emphasized that language shapes thought, and thought shapes belief. Gregory of Nazianzus, in his *Theological Orations*, labored over the precision of theological language, recognizing that error in speech often led to error in doctrine.[6] Augustine similarly stressed the moral weight of words, noting that they must reflect divine truth, discerned through faith and reason, to avoid leading souls astray.[7]

In the debates over Christological and Trinitarian formulations at Nicaea (325) and Chalcedon (451), the careful crafting of terms like *homoousios* ("of the same substance") and *hypostasis* was not merely semantic.[8] These debates demonstrate the church's understanding that socially constructed language must be accountable to revealed truth, apprehended through faith and reason. The Holy Spirit, as the agent of divine guidance, empowers the Church to speak truthfully, aligning human language with God's Logos (John 16:13).

Martin Luther's emphasis on *sola scriptura* was about recovering a biblical vocabulary capable of reforming distorted constructs.[9] John Calvin's *Institutes* demonstrate how language, when saturated with Scripture and informed by faith and reason, can reform theological discourse and societal ethics.[10] The Enlightenment shifted toward autonomous human reason as the arbiter of meaning, relativizing theological language. Postmodernity challenged this but often embraced radical subjectivity. The *ekklesia* must reclaim the formative role of divinely inspired language, guided by the Spirit, faith, and reason to reflect God's truth (Rom 1:20; Heb 11:3).

Language, when submitted to divine revelation, becomes sacramental—it participates in and conveys grace. When cut off from its theological roots, it risks being co-opted by ideologies that distort God's order, evident in contested terms like "identity," "justice," and "truth." The *ekklesia* must remain vigilant in guarding and reforming its lexicon.

6. Gregory of Nazianzus, *Theological Orations*, 29–30.
7. Augustine, *City of God*, trans. Bettenson, 15.27 (580–81).
8. Pelikan, *Christian Tradition*, 200–205.
9. Luther, *On Christian Liberty*, 10–12.
10. Calvin, *Institutes*, 2.4.1.

IMPLICATIONS FOR MORAL EPISTEMOLOGY AND NATURAL LAW

The social construction of reality intersects with moral epistemology—the study of how we know right from wrong. From a biblical perspective, moral truths are discovered, not invented, embedded in the created order and apprehended through faith and reason (Rom 1:20). The doctrine of natural law affirms this, with Paul noting that even gentiles "show that the requirements of the law are written on their hearts" (Rom 2:14–15). Sin, however, distorts perception, fracturing our ability to discern moral truth.[11]

Natural law posits a moral grammar to the universe, accessible to human reason but authored by God and confirmed by faith. Thomas Aquinas wrote that the natural law is "nothing else than the rational creature's participation in the eternal law."[12] Modern constructivist approaches often deny moral universals, arguing that ethics are products of culture and power. This relativism cannot justify moral judgments against oppression or injustice without a transcultural standard. Natural law, informed by faith and reason, provides such a framework (Heb 11:3).

Moral epistemology must remain accountable to general revelation (nature and conscience) and special revelation (Scripture). Psalm 19 demonstrates this twofold witness:

> The heavens tell of the glory of God. . . . The law of the Lord is perfect, restoring the soul. (Ps 19:1, 7)

Social constructions that reject moral absolutes undermine justice and human dignity. Christians are called to discern reality through the "renewing of the mind" (Rom 12:2) and to test all things against God's revealed character, using faith and reason.

CONTEMPORARY APPLICATIONS AND THEOLOGICAL CHALLENGES

In today's cultural climate, the notion that truth and identity are socially constructed permeates education, politics, law, and religion. Christian theology insists that reality is disclosed by God, not created ex nihilo by

---

11. Plantinga, *Not the Way*, 100–105.
12. Aquinas, *Summa Theologica*, I-II, Q91, A2.

society. Christ's atoning work redeems our fractured epistemology, restoring our capacity to interpret reality in alignment with divine truth, through faith and reason (Col 1:15-20; Heb 11:3).

Issues such as gender identity and the redefinition of marriage reflect attempts to construct meaning apart from creation's order, mirroring Babel's autonomy (Gen 11:1-9). Scripture and natural law affirm that freedom operates within the boundaries of design (Gen 1:27; Rom 1:20-27). Eschatologically, the social construction of reality finds its fulfillment in the new creation, where human constructs are redeemed and aligned with God's purpose (Rev 21:1-5).

The church must engage in loving but firm apologetics, articulating human flourishing grounded in divine intent. This includes reclaiming biblical language, challenging relativism, and embodying communities where truth and grace are held in tension (John 1:14). A pressing challenge is discipling believers who have absorbed postmodern assumptions. The pastoral task involves epistemological reformation, taking "every thought captive to obey Christ" (2 Cor 10:5).

This chapter calls for a renewed theological anthropology—one that sees humans as image-bearers called into communion with the Logos. In him, reality is not only constructed but revealed, redeemed, and restored through the interplay of faith and reason (Col 1:15-20; Rom 1:20; Heb 11:3).

3

Sin
A Theological Framework

SIN IS COMMONLY UNDERSTOOD as transgression of God's law, a broken relationship with him, or missing the mark of his holiness (1 John 3:4; Isa 59:2; Rom 3:23). While these definitions are biblically grounded, they often reduce sin to acts of omission (failing to do what is commanded) or commission (doing what is forbidden). Such reductionism obscures sin's deeper root: evil, a capricious and pervasive force that distorts God's created order in unpredictable ways. The present framework argues that sin, as the ubiquitous extension of evil, manifests in five distinct yet interconnected ways: omission, commission, physical/biological, metaphysical, and transcendent. These manifestations reveal sin's insidious, erratic, and all-encompassing nature, infiltrating every dimension of existence.

Drawing on biblical theology, historical theology, and systematic theology, this chapter develops a robust hamartiology, comparing the proposed framework with traditional views and assessing its novelty. It concludes with seven reasons why understanding sin's breadth and capriciousness is vital, emphasizing its implications for humility, redemption, and dependence on God's grace to counter its unpredictable reach.

BIBLICAL THEOLOGY OF SIN

Scripture portrays sin as a multifaceted, capricious force rooted in evil. In the Old Testament, sin is described as transgression (*pesha*; e.g., Isa 53:5, 12) and rebellion (*chatta'ah* is better understood as "missing the mark"; e.g., Gen 39:9). The New Testament builds on these concepts, defining sin as lawlessness (1 John 3:4) and universal falling short (Rom 3:23). Genesis 3 narrates sin's entry through Adam and Eve's disobedience, unpredictably fracturing relationships with God, self, others, and creation (Gen 3:1–19). The curse on the ground (Gen 3:17–19) and creation's groaning (Rom 8:19–22) illustrate sin's erratic impact on the physical world, suggesting a physical/biological dimension. Romans 5:12–21 universalizes sin's scope, infiltrating all humanity through Adam, while Rom 1:18–32 depicts sin as a volatile rejection of God's truth, leading to moral and spiritual chaos.

Jesus expands sin's reach to thoughts and intentions (Matt 5:21–28), revealing its capricious presence in the metaphysical realm of the heart and mind (cf. Jer 17:9; Ps 139:23–24). Paul's concept of the "flesh" (*sarx*) in Rom 7:18–25 portrays sin as an indwelling, unpredictable force, potentially aligning with a physical/biological manifestation. Ephesians 6:12 and Col 2:15 point to cosmic powers of evil, suggesting a transcendent dimension that operates beyond human or even satanic control, subject only to God's sovereignty (cf. Job 1–2). The capricious nature of sin is evident in its ability to distort reality at every level, from the material to the cosmic, requiring divine intervention to restrain its erratic influence.

HISTORICAL THEOLOGY OF SIN

Historical theology reveals diverse perspectives on sin's nature, often highlighting its unpredictable character. Augustine's doctrine of original sin, articulated in *City of God* and *Confessions*, posits that sin is inherited from Adam, corrupting human nature and will in erratic ways (*peccatum originale*).[1] He views evil as a privation of good (*privatio boni*),[2] a chaotic force that unpredictably distorts God's order, aligning

---

1. Augustine, *City of God*, trans. Bettenson, 13.14 (570–71); Augustine, *Confessions*, 110–12.

2. Augustine, *Enchiridion*, 11.4.

with the proposed framework's emphasis on sin as an extension of evil. Pelagius, Augustine's contemporary, argued that humans retain free will to avoid sin, a view condemned at the Council of Carthage (418) for underestimating sin's pervasive and capricious grip.[3]

Medieval theologians like Thomas Aquinas defined sin as an act contrary to divine law, focusing on omission and commission but not explicitly addressing its physical or metaphysical volatility.[4] The reformers Luther and Calvin emphasized sin's totality. Luther's *Bondage of the Will* portrays humanity as enslaved to sin's erratic power, while Calvin's *Institutes* describes total depravity, highlighting sin's unpredictable corruption of every faculty.[5] In the modern era, Karl Barth's concept of "nothingness" (*das Nichtige*) frames sin as an irrational, chaotic opposition to God's grace, resonating with the transcendent category of the present framework by suggesting a force beyond human control.[6] Irenaeus's view of sin as a cosmic disruption further supports its capricious, far-reaching nature.[7]

SYSTEMATIC THEOLOGY OF SIN

Systematic theology synthesizes sin as both act and state, often emphasizing its unpredictable pervasiveness. Wayne Grudem defines sin as "any failure to conform to the moral law of God in act, attitude, or nature," capturing its erratic scope across human existence.[8] Millard Erickson distinguishes between original sin (inherited corruption) and actual sin (personal acts), focusing on omission and commission but less on sin's volatile presence in material or metaphysical realms.[9] Cornelius Plantinga's *Not the Way It's Supposed to Be* describes sin as a "vandalism of shalom," a disruptive force rooted in evil that unpredictably fractures God's order, aligning closely with the proposed framework.[10]

---

3. Pelikan, *Christian Tradition*, 313–18.
4. Aquinas, *Summa Theologica*, I–II, Q71, A6.
5. Luther, *Bondage of the Will*, 137–40; Calvin, *Institutes*, 2.1.8.
6. Barth, *Church Dogmatics*, 3/3, 289–368.
7. Irenaeus, *Against Heresies*, 551-51.
8. Grudem, *Systematic Theology*, 490.
9. Erickson, *Christian Theology*, 582–95.
10. Plantinga, *Not the Way*, 10–13.

Alister McGrath integrates psychological and sociological dimensions, viewing sin as a distortion of identity and relationships, which supports the metaphysical category of this hamartiology by highlighting its capricious influence on the mind.[11] G. C. Berkouwer sees sin as a power that enslaves humanity, requiring divine redemption, which echoes the transcendent category, though it typically attributes evil to demonic forces rather than a force beyond Satan.[12] The present framework is novel in explicitly categorizing sin's manifestations and emphasizing its capricious nature as an extension of evil, particularly in the physical/biological, metaphysical, and transcendent dimensions.

FIVE MANIFESTATIONS OF SIN

Building on biblical and theological insights, the proposed framework describes sin as a capricious extension of evil, manifesting in five ways:

- **Omission:** Failing to do what God commands, reflecting evil's subtle neglect of divine will (Jas 4:17).
- **Commission:** Doing what is forbidden, embodying evil's overt rebellion (1 John 3:4).
- **Physical/biological:** Sin's erratic presence in physical matter, evident in creation's groaning and the cursed ground (Rom 8:19–22; Gen 3:17–19).
- **Metaphysical:** Sin's unpredictable infiltration of thought life, intuition, and dreams, as seen in Jesus' teaching on internal sin (Matt 5:21–28; Jer 17:9).
- **Transcendent:** Sin as a cosmic force, capriciously eclipsing even Satan's control and requiring God's sovereign intervention (Eph 6:12; Job 1–2; Col 2:15).

These manifestations reveal sin's insidious, erratic nature, rooted in evil's chaotic distortion of God's creation. While omission and commission are traditional, the physical/biological, metaphysical, and transcendent categories are novel, highlighting sin's unpredictable reach across material, psychological, and cosmic realms.

11. McGrath, *Scientific Theology*, 195–200.
12. Berkouwer, *Sin*, 245–60.

IMPLICATIONS AND IMPORTANCE

Understanding sin's breadth and capriciousness as an extension of evil has seven key implications for theological reflection and Christian practice:

1. It frees believers from the illusion that sin's erratic nature can be controlled through effort alone, emphasizing reliance on grace (Rom 5:20–21).
2. It discourages judgmentalism based on performative achievements, as sin's unpredictability affects all (Rom 2:1–3).
3. It provides a lens to understand the world's chaotic brokenness, from environmental crises to mental turmoil (Rom 8:19–22).
4. It deepens appreciation for Christ's victory over sin's volatile power (Col 2:15; 1 Cor 15:57).
5. It fosters respect for the Holy Spirit's work in restraining sin's capricious influence (Rom 8:13).
6. It inclines believers to seek daily grace to navigate sin's unpredictable effects (Lam 3:22–23).
7. It underscores the need for hope in God's ultimate triumph over sin's chaos, as "the substance of things hoped for" (Heb 11:1).

CONCLUSION

The proposed framework offers a novel hamartiology by categorizing sin as a capricious extension of evil, manifesting in omission, commission, physical/biological, metaphysical, and transcendent forms. It challenges reductionist views, emphasizing sin's unpredictable pervasiveness across all dimensions of existence. The church must proclaim this comprehensive understanding to foster humility, awe at Christ's redemption, and dependence on the Spirit to counter sin's erratic reach, aligning human life with God's sovereign order (Col 2:15; Job 1–2).

4

The Radical Nature of God's Love

A POPULAR SONG FROM the 1980s raised the question as to whether we really even comprehend love. Human conceptions of love—shaped by sentiment, biology, and social constructs—pale against the radical love of God, a love so profound it eludes those not illuminated by his Spirit. This chapter contends that God's love, rooted in his very nature (1 John 4:8), is not merely an attribute but the animating force of creation, holiness, redemption, sacrifice, liberation, transformation, and restoration. Unlike human love, defined from a bottom-up perspective through incomplete experiences, God's love demands a top-down surrender to his definition, revealed through Scripture and experienced in the believer's life. This love, hidden yet evident, is obscured by the adversary's distortions and our desensitization, yet it permeates existence, from the coded complexity of DNA to the soul's enduring imprint. To grasp it, we must lay our assumptions on the altar of humility, embracing faith as the lens to see what materialism blinds us to.

THE HIDDEN YET EVIDENT LOVE OF GOD

God's radical love is both ubiquitous and elusive, like a melody heard faintly amid life's cacophony. It is hidden not by divine concealment but by our socially conditioned lenses, steeped in materialism and sentimentality, which distort its reality. The adversary exploits this, crafting counterfeit love that hijacks biological and emotional impulses while suppressing spiritual and cognitive capacities. By portraying God as stern or unjust, evil obscures his love and diminishes our value as image-bearers (Gen 1:26–27). Yet, this love shines in creation's design, the moral law written on our hearts, and Christ's transformative sacrifice. To apprehend it, we must reject materialist assumptions that only sensory evidence constitutes reality, a view rooted in Enlightenment empiricism.[1] As Augustine observed, faith enables understanding of divine truths beyond empirical limits.[2]

Two observations frame our exploration: first, God's love is woven into existence's fabric, hidden in plain sight; second, without recognizing our value as God's image-bearers, we cannot grasp its depth. The adversary's strategy is to obscure this love and devalue humanity through cultural homogeneity and distorted narratives of God's character. Our task is to dismantle these distortions through seven expressions of God's love: creation, holiness, redemption, sacrifice, liberation, transformation, and restoration.

CREATION: THE FIRST ACT OF RADICAL LOVE

God's love precedes human constructs of affection, originating in creation itself. Genesis 1:1 declares, "In the beginning God created the heavens and the earth," an act of divine will rooted in love (1 John 4:8). Revelation 4:11 affirms,

> "You are worthy, our Lord and God, to receive glory and honor and power; for You created all things, and because of Your will they existed, and were created."

The semantic range of "will"—encompassing purpose, desire, and delight—links creation to divine love. Creation is not random but a deliberate expression of a loving mind, contra materialist claims of a universe

---

1. Hume, *Enquiry Concerning Human Understanding*, 108–12.
2. Augustine, *Confessions*, 7.10 (123–25).

without purpose.³ From gravity's precision to DNA's 67 billion miles of coded instructions, creation testifies to a purposeful intelligence.⁴

This love is radical because it exists independently of human recognition, predating social bonds. The ecosystem's interdependency—plants sustaining air, animals cycling nutrients, humans cultivating the earth—reflects divine design for flourishing (Gen 2:15). Materialism, celebrating the universe's "magical" existence while denying a creator, fails to account for this order. For believers, creation's laws are love's material evidence, discernible through faith. We must reject sentimentalism that reduces love to instinct and embrace the truth that "God is love" (1 John 4:8).

HOLINESS: LOVE SET APART AND PURPOSEFUL

God's holiness—his set-apartness and purposefulness—reveals his radical love. As Creator and Lawgiver, God established boundaries to safeguard flourishing. In Gen 2:16-17, he commanded Adam,

> "From any tree of the garden you may freely eat; but from the tree of the knowledge of good and evil you shall not eat, for on the day that you eat from it you will certainly die."

This prohibition was protective, ensuring holiness through obedience. The text implies Adam and Eve's understanding of death, as God's justice would not impose an incomprehensible consequence. The Hebrew phrase "dying you will die" suggests a progression from spiritual to physical death, aligning with creation's cycles (Gen 8:22).

Humanity's set-apartness mirrors God's holiness. Created in his image (Gen 1:26-27), humans are distinguished by roles—male and female, doctors and artists—contributing to societal flourishing. This diversity reflects divine love, yet sin's fracture obscures it. God's provision for restoration, planned before the fall (Rev 13:8), underscores his love's radical nature. Alvin Plantinga argues that belief in God's purposeful design is "properly basic," grounded in creation's evident order.⁵

---

3. Walton, *Lost World*, 112-15.
4. Collins, *Language of God*, 124-26.
5. Plantinga, *Warranted Christian Belief*, 167-98.

REDEMPTION: LOVE AS KINSMAN-REDEEMER

Redemption epitomizes God's radical love, delivering humanity from sin's slavery. Romans 5:8-9 states,

> God demonstrates His own love toward us, in that while we were yet sinners, Christ died for us. . . . [H]aving now been justified by His blood, we shall be saved from the wrath of God through Him.

The Greek term for redemption, from *ek* (out of) and *agorazo* (to buy), means purchasing from slavery, while the Hebrew *go'el* (kinsman-redeemer) signifies delivering to sustain a bloodline (Lev 25:47-55). Christ, as purchaser and kinsman, frees believers from wrath, law, sin, and death, embodying justice and love.

This redemption is radical, addressing inherited guilt through Adam's sin (Rom 5:12). Unlike materialist views reducing morality to evolutionary instincts, redemption reveals a spiritual law written on the heart (Rom 2:14-15), perceptible through faith. God's love, expressed in Christ's death, depends on his grace, not our merit (Eph 1:7-8).

SACRIFICE: LOVE IN SUBSTITUTION

Sacrifice is the experiential core of God's love. Second Corinthians 5:21 declares,

> He made Him who knew no sin to be sin in our behalf, so that we might become the righteousness of God in Him.

Christ's death was spiritual, bearing humanity's sin (1 Pet 2:24). Isaiah 52:14 and 50:6 describe his suffering, yet sin, not wounds, killed him. This substitution—Christ taking humanity's place—fulfills justice while enabling righteousness, a radical act transcending human sacrifice.

Sacrifice is not static but lived, involving God's surrender of his Son and Christ's endurance of evil. This love challenges human fairness, demanding forgiveness and empathy.

LIBERATION: LOVE AS FREEDOM

Liberation, implied in redemption, frees believers from sin's bondage, aligning with God's purpose for flourishing. Galatians 5:1—"It was for freedom that Christ set us free"—suggests liberation as love's facet. This freedom is not license but empowerment to live according to God's design, overcoming the adversary's distortions.

TRANSFORMATION: LOVE'S EVIDENCE IN CHANGED LIVES

Transformed lives are compelling evidence of God's love. Unlike materialist science limiting evidence to sensory data, transformation is observable through cognitive and behavioral changes (Gal 6:1–5). A taxonomy of transformation—gradual, instant, episodic—captures its diversity, as in Saul's conversion (Acts 9:1–19). These changes, measurable through testimony, transcend materialist skepticism.[6] Isaiah 64:6 reminds us, "All our righteous deeds are like a filthy garment," yet God's love persists, inviting confession (Jas 5:16) for healing, not shame. This love transforms us toward holiness despite brokenness.

RESTORATION: LOVE'S ULTIMATE AIM

Restoration returns creation to its intended state. Categories like captivity (2 Chr 7:14), restitution (Luke 19:8–9), healing (Luke 5:18–25), and repair (Ezra 9:10) illustrate the scope of transformation it requires. Revelation 22:3–5 envisions a restored creation where "there will no longer be any curse." This symbiotic relationship reflects divine love, reversing sin's fracture.

FORGIVENESS: THE SOUL OF GOD'S LOVE

Forgiveness is the heartbeat of God's love. In Matt 18:21–35, Jesus' parable of the unforgiving servant shows that God's forgiveness of our unpayable debt requires us to forgive others. Christ's plea, "Father, forgive them; for they do not know what they are doing" (Luke 23:34), roots forgiveness in human ignorance (Gen 3:1–4). Forgiveness demands empathy—cognitive, emotional, compassionate—challenging avoidance or

---

6. Creswell, *Research Design*, 185–90.

denial (Eph 4:31–32). Jesus' command to forgive "seventy times seven" (Matt 18:22) underscores its divine nature.

THE MYSTERIES OF GOD'S LOVE

God's love is shrouded in mystery due to sin's fracture (Gen 3:1–4). Four mysteries—evil and suffering, consciousness, existence, and love—reveal its radical nature.

1. **Evil and suffering:** Evil exists due to free will, essential for love (1 John 4:8). Suffering serves a redemptive purpose, immunizing against rebellion (Phil 2:10–11).
2. **Consciousness:** Consciousness enables moral responsibility and awareness of God (Rom 1:18–20). Its metaphysical nature points to divine love.
3. **Existence:** The soul-print ensures continuity beyond entropy (Ps 139:16; Eccl 12:7). Resurrection restores this imprint (1 Cor 15:42–44).
4. **Love:** Sin made love a mystery, but Christ's incarnation reveals it (John 1:14). Full understanding awaits communion (Rev 22:3–5).

   Faith, not empiricism, unveils God's love (Heb 11:3).

CONCLUSION: LIVING GOD'S RADICAL LOVE

To know God's love is to live it. Salvation is free, but understanding requires costly participation—sharing Christ's suffering and compassion (1 John 4:12). The biblical narrative is a messy yet purposeful love story. Psalm 34:18 assures, "The Lord is near to the brokenhearted." God's love will be fully revealed when the mystery is finished (Rev 10:6–7).

5

Divine Love vs. Human, Socially Constructed Love

THIS CHAPTER EXPLORES THE ontological contrast between divine love—rooted in God's holy nature—and socially constructed love that emerges from the devolving social culture apart from divine revelation. The love that contemporary society takes comfort in bears many of the characteristics of divine love. It values fidelity, compassion, empathy, affection, passion, and many of the familiar virtues associated with love, yet it is distorted because it is untethered from the Source of love. Divine love is holy, i.e., set apart and purposeful, and is applied covenantally. It contains within itself justice, mercy, and truth, never compromising one for the other. Human, socially constructed love, by contrast, tends to elevate individual desire and mutual consent as supreme values—often at the expense of holiness and ontological purpose. This chapter will unfold the biblical contours of divine love, contrast them with human constructions, explore implications for ethics and ecclesiology, and engage key thinkers from Augustine to modern critics.

BIBLICAL FOUNDATIONS OF DIVINE LOVE

Scripture declares that love is God's essence: "God is love" (1 John 4:8, 16), a metaphysical truth revealing his holy nature (set apart and purposeful). This love manifests in creation's goodness (Gen 1:31), redemption's sacrifice—"God so loved the world, that He gave His only Son" (John 3:16)—and eschatological fulfillment, where the *ekklesia* is sanctified as Christ's Bride (Eph 5:27). The Hebrew *ḥesed*, God's steadfast covenant love, endures despite Israel's rebellion: "I have loved you with an everlasting love" (Jer 31:3). This *ḥesed*, untranslatable yet rich with fidelity, reflects God's purposeful commitment, set apart from human merit (Ps 136:1).

Paul describes this holy love as *agapē*—unconditional, volitional, and self-emptying (Rom 5:8; 1 Cor 13:4–7). It transforms believers: "The love of Christ controls us" (2 Cor 5:14), compelling us to holiness, set apart for God's purpose (1 Pet 1:15–16). Unlike human love, which often indulges desire, divine love redeems without endorsing sin (Titus 3:4–7).

THEOLOGICAL NATURE OF DIVINE LOVE

Divine love flows from God's holiness (*qadosh*, set apart and purposeful), never arbitrary but covenantally ordered (Lev 19:2; Isa 6:3). R. C. Sproul observes,

> God's love constitutes not so much an emotion as a holy disposition acting in perfect consistency with His righteous character.[1]

It balances justice and mercy (Exod 34:6–7), disciplining rather than indulging, as J. I. Packer notes: "God's love disciplines rather than indulges" (Heb 12:6). Augustine teaches that true love orders desires toward God, the source of all good (1 John 4:10).[2]

Karl Barth frames divine love as God's righteous freedom, expressed in Christ's self-giving (John 14:15), making believers "partakers of the divine nature" (2 Pet 1:4).[3] This love, set apart and purposeful, seeks the beloved's restoration, never compromising truth.

---

1. Sproul, *Holiness of God*, 57–59.
2. Augustine, *Confessions*, 7.10 (123–25).
3. Barth, *Church Dogmatics*, 2/1, 735.

HISTORICAL DEVELOPMENT OF LOVE'S CONCEPT

Love's distortion traces a historical arc. Aristotle's *philia* prioritized friendship, while medieval theology blended *agapē* and *eros*, often obscuring divine love's holy purpose.[4] Luther's "theology of the cross" reclaimed love as theological, rooted in Christ's sacrifice, not cultural ideals (1 Cor 13:6).[5] The Enlightenment, as Charles Taylor notes, severed love from revelation, prioritizing subjective happiness over covenantal fidelity.[6] Carl Trueman identifies modernity's "psychologized expressivism," where love becomes self-expression, not self-giving (Rom 1:25).[7] Jean Twenge highlights how social media amplifies this, substituting digital "likes" for covenantal care.[8] Bonhoeffer warns,

> If you board the wrong train, no amount of running in the opposite direction will help.[9]

This shadow of love, devoid of holiness (set apart and purposeful), deceives by mimicking commitment without God's design.

SOCIALLY CONSTRUCTED LOVE: AN EXPANDED DEFINITION

Human love, untethered from God, is a cultural mirage, bearing virtues like fidelity yet lacking divine purpose. Socially constructed love posits that romantic and interpersonal love is not universal but shaped by cultural, historical, and ideological forces. Michel Foucault argues that love is a discourse regulated by power, where societal norms dictate its legitimacy.[10] Niklas Luhmann traces its codification during the Enlightenment, shifting from duty to individualistic fulfillment.[11] Eva Illouz's "emotional capitalism" reveals love as commodified, governed

---

4. Lewis, *Four Loves*, 7–12.
5. Luther, "Freedom of a Christian," 349–50.
6. Taylor, *Sources of the Self*, 211–15.
7. Trueman, *Rise and Triumph*, 188–92.
8. Twenge, *iGen*, 78–82.
9. Bonhoeffer, *Ethics*, 67.
10. Foucault, *History of Sexuality*, 43–44.
11. Luhmann, *Love as Passion*, 15–18.

by cost-benefit logic in dating apps and wedding industries.[12] Zygmunt Bauman's *Liquid Love* describes it as fragile, reflecting consumer culture's preference for instant gratification.[13]

Judith Butler critiques love's regulation by heteronormative norms, marginalizing queer or polyamorous expressions, while Laura Kipnis sees it as enforcing conformity through monogamy.[14] Media's "happily ever after" tropes, as Jean Twenge notes, reduce love to performative affirmation.[15] Critics like Helen Fisher argue this view overlooks biological roots (e.g., oxytocin-driven bonding), yet its Western-centric focus risks ignoring non-Western kinship systems.[16] As bell hooks asserts, love is a verb—an active, participatory choice that can challenge oppressive norms when rooted in truth.[17]

THE BRIDE AND COVENANT LOVE

Christ's love for the *ekklesia*, his bride, is divine love's supreme archetype:

> Husbands, love your wives, as Christ loved the church. (Eph 5:25)

Rooted in Yahweh's fidelity to Israel (Hos 2:14–20; Jer 3:6–10), this love sanctifies despite unfaithfulness (Rev 19:7–9). Jürgen Moltmann's cruciform theology highlights how Christ's cross embodies this transformative, holy love (set apart and purposeful).[18] The *ekklesia*, formed by divine calling, not cultural consensus, reflects God's purposeful commitment.

POLEMICAL CHALLENGES AND PASTORAL RESPONSE

Contemporary culture frames love as uncritical inclusion, asking, "What's wrong with love if it's consensual?" Yet, this misses holiness (set apart and purposeful), the core of divine love (1 Cor 13:6). Stanley

---

12. Illouz, *Cold Intimacies*, 45–50.
13. Bauman, *Liquid Love*, viii–x.
14. Butler, *Gender Trouble*, 112–15; Kipnis, *Against Love*, 25–30.
15. Twenge, *iGen*, 78–82.
16. Fisher, *Why We Love*, 85–90.
17. hooks, *All About Love*, 4–5.
18. Moltmann, *Crucified God*, 243–45.

Grenz warns that love without moral order enslaves rather than liberates.[19] The *ekklesia* must meet people where they are, as Christ did at Jacob's well (John 4:7–26), speaking truth in love (Eph 4:15). We are called to offer grace without affirming sin (John 8:11), trusting God's kindness to lead to repentance (Rom 2:4).

CONCLUSION

Divine love, like a river from God's holy heart (set apart and purposeful), flows with covenantal fidelity, while socially constructed love, a cultural mirage, deceives with shadows. The *ekklesia* must reclaim a love rooted in Christ's sacrifice, set apart for God's purpose. Let us listen for the Shepherd's voice, rejecting human scripts that obscure his grace, and embody a love that sanctifies in a morally confused age.

---

19. Grenz, *Moral Quest*, 253.

6

Rereading Divorce from the Big Picture
A Theological Reappraisal of Covenant, Judgment, and Grace

THE THEOLOGICAL REAPPRAISAL OF divorce articulated in this work centers on God's actions in redemptive history, which reveal the interplay of covenant, judgment, and grace in his dealings with Israel, Judah, and the *ekklesia*. For instance, in Hos 2:14–20, God judges Israel's covenantal unfaithfulness by sending her away, yet promises to allure her back with kindness, demonstrating judgment tempered by grace within a renewed covenant.[1] This chapter extends this reappraisal by explicitly emphasizing that God's actions—his divorce of both Israel and Judah, his establishment of the *ekklesia* as the bride of Christ, and his realistic portrayal of human marriage—provide a coherent framework for understanding divorce, addressing widespread confusion among Bible-believing Christians and challenging misreadings that oversimplify or condemn it. This vision, rooted in divine faithfulness, prophetic justice, and ecclesial grace, offers a covenantally grounded perspective that is both holy and honest.

---

1. Stuart, *Hosea-Jonah*, 52–54.

THE DIVINE PRECEDENT OF DIVORCE

Biblical divorce, as modeled in Scripture, is a covenantal and judicial act dissolving a marriage due to grave violations such as idolatry or adultery, as seen in God's issuance of a "certificate of divorce" to Israel (Jer 3:8), and permitted under Mosaic law for indecency (Deut 24:1–4). This definition clarifies that divorce, when aligned with covenantal principles, addresses serious breaches of fidelity, reflecting divine justice rather than capriciousness.

There remains widespread confusion among Bible-believing Christians concerning divorce, often driven by a misreading of Mal 2:16—"For I hate divorce, says the LORD, the God of Israel"—taken out of context to condemn all divorce. As Walter Kaiser notes, the text condemns treachery in divorce, particularly among priests who abandoned faithful Jewish wives for pagan women, not the act itself when necessitated by covenantal betrayal.[2] This misunderstanding obscures the moral and redemptive dynamics of God's own actions, which provide a clearer lens for understanding divorce.

Jeremiah's prophecy leaves no room for allegorical interpretation:

> "And I saw that for all the adulteries of faithless Israel, I had sent her away and given her a certificate of divorce." (Jer 3:8)

The Hebrew terminology here is precise and legally binding—*shalach* ("sent away") and *sefer keritut* ("certificate of divorce") directly mirrors the language of divorce legislation in Deut 24:1.[3] This is no mere metaphor, but a divine judicial act with real covenantal consequences.

Adultery is wrong because it violates the covenantal fidelity that mirrors God's exclusive relationship with his people, equating to faithlessness, as seen in Israel's idolatry (Ezek 16:32; Hos 4:12). This betrayal not only breaks trust but also imperils the covenant community by fostering division and moral corruption, as God's divorce of Israel and Judah illustrates. The connection to faithlessness underscores why such breaches warrant divine judgment, as they disrupt the communal and spiritual order intended by the covenant.[4]

---

2. Kaiser, *Toward Old Testament Ethics*, 67–68.
3. Brown et al., *Hebrew and English Lexicon*, 1018, 503.
4. Wenham, *Story as Torah*, 78–80.

Jesus' teachings on divorce further illuminate this connection, emphasizing that adultery stems from a deeper faithlessness rooted in "hardness of heart." In Matt 19:3–6, when questioned by the Pharisees about divorce, Jesus points to the creation ideal:

> "Have you not read that He who created them from the beginning made them male and female, and said, 'For this reason a man shall leave his father and his mother and be joined to his wife, and the two shall become one flesh'? So they are no longer two, but one flesh. Therefore, what God has joined together, no person is to separate."

He acknowledges that Moses permitted divorce "because of your hardness of heart," but clarifies, "from the beginning it has not been this way" (Matt 19:8). This "hardness of heart" represents a faithless resistance to God's covenantal design, where adultery not only severs marital unity but also reflects a spiritual unfaithfulness akin to idolatry, undermining the covenant's reflection of God's steadfast love.[5] Jesus permits divorce for *porneia* (sexual immorality, including adultery), recognizing that such faithlessness can irreparably rend the marriage bond, yet his indictment highlights the root issue: a heart resistant to God's original intent for faithful union.[6]

Leading theological scholars affirm the role of faith in marriage as a covenant of mutual fidelity that mirrors Christ's faithful relationship with the *ekklesia*, while portraying faithlessness in adultery as a profound betrayal of trust and divine order. N. T. Wright emphasizes that marriage embodies God's faithful covenant with humanity, where faith sustains the "one flesh" union as a witness to divine loyalty; adultery, in this view, is faithlessness because it fractures this sacred reflection, prioritizing self over covenantal commitment.[7] Similarly, Timothy Keller describes marriage as a "gospel reenactment," where faith in God's promises fosters sacrificial love and intimacy; adultery betrays this faith, introducing distrust and severing the bond that faith nurtures.[8] David Instone-Brewer, focusing on biblical contexts, notes that adultery's wrongness lies in its violation of covenantal exclusivity, a faithlessness

---

5. Blomberg, *Matthew*, 290–92.
6. Instone-Brewer, *Divorce and Remarriage in the Church*, 134–36.
7. Wright, *Paul and the Faithfulness*, 1012–15.
8. Keller and Keller, *Meaning of Marriage*, 112–15.

that mirrors Israel's unfaithfulness to God, eroding the trust essential to marital and communal stability.⁹ John Piper highlights faith's role in empowering covenant-keeping, arguing that adultery arises from a faithless heart that idolizes desire over God's commands, disrupting the marital portrayal of Christ's unwavering love for the church.[10] These insights collectively underscore that faith is the sustaining force in marriage, enabling fidelity and intimacy, while adultery embodies faithlessness, not merely as moral failure but as a covenantal rupture with spiritual and communal consequences.[11] While adultery represents a direct form of covenantal breach, the complexities of divorce extend to other expressions of faithlessness, such as abandonment, which Paul addresses in 1 Cor 7 as legitimate grounds for separation, further illustrating the role of faith in sustaining marriage.

THE COMPLEXITIES OF DIVORCE: ABANDONMENT AS COVENANT BREACH

In 1 Cor 7:10–16, Paul provides practical counsel on marriage and divorce, emphasizing the complexities introduced by mixed marriages between believers and unbelievers. He instructs married couples not to divorce:

> But to the married I give instructions, not I, but the Lord, that the wife is not to leave her husband (but if she does leave, she must remain unmarried, or else be reconciled to her husband), and that the husband is not to divorce his wife. (1 Cor 7:10–11)

However, Paul introduces an exception for abandonment:

> Yet if the unbelieving one is leaving, let him leave; the brother or the sister is not under bondage in such cases, but God has called us in peace. (1 Cor 7:15)

Here, abandonment by an unbeliever is portrayed as a form of adulterating the marriage covenant, as it breaks the bond of mutual commitment and peace, effectively deserting the faithful partner and imperiling the covenantal relationship. Paul's counsel recognizes the reality of human faithlessness, allowing the believer freedom—"not

---

9. Instone-Brewer, *Divorce and Remarriage in the Bible*, 200–202.
10. Piper, *This Momentary Marriage*, 85–87.
11. Piper, *This Momentary Marriage*, 89–91.

enslaved"—from the marriage bond in cases of abandonment, while prioritizing reconciliation where possible and peace in the face of irreconcilable breach.

Noted Pauline scholars affirm that abandonment in 1 Cor 7:15 constitutes a covenant breach akin to adultery, releasing the believer from the marriage and permitting remarriage, as it reflects a faithless rejection of the covenant's relational demands. Gordon D. Fee, in his commentary on 1 Corinthians, interprets "not enslaved" (*ou dedoulotai*) as meaning the believer is no longer bound to the marriage, free to remarry after abandonment, emphasizing that Paul's exception addresses the practical complexities of faithlessness in mixed marriages, where the unbeliever's departure disrupts the covenantal unity intended by God.[12] Anthony C. Thiselton similarly views abandonment as dissolving the marriage bond, arguing that Paul's language of "peace" underscores the covenant's relational nature, where faith sustains harmony; abandonment embodies faithlessness by rejecting this peace, allowing the believer release without guilt.[13] David E. Garland highlights that Paul's counsel reflects the covenantal principle of mutual fidelity, with abandonment as a faithless act that imperils the marriage's stability, granting freedom to the abandoned spouse as a concession to human hardness of heart.[14] Richard B. Hays notes that Paul's exception for abandonment recognizes the covenant's fragility in the face of unbelief, connecting it to faithlessness as a breach of God's design for marriage as a reflection of Christ's faithful union with the church.[15]

Paul's instructions in 1 Cor 7:10–11 make clear that abandonment by a believing spouse represents a greater adulteration of the marriage covenant than abandonment by an unbeliever, as it directly violates the Lord's command for believers to maintain marital unity and reflects a profound faithlessness within the body of Christ. Leading Pauline scholars emphasize that for believing spouses, divorce or abandonment is strictly prohibited, with separation (if it occurs) requiring the spouses to remain unmarried or reconcile, underscoring the severity of such a breach in a covenant sanctified by faith. Gordon D. Fee argues

---

12. Fee, *First Epistle*, 303–6.
13. Thiselton, *First Epistle*, 532–35.
14. Garland, *1 Corinthians*, 288–90.
15. Hays, *First Corinthians*, 120–22.

that Paul's command in 1 Cor 7:10-11 is binding on believers because it echoes Jesus' teaching (Matt 19:3-9), viewing abandonment by a believer as a sin against the Christian community, imperiling the witness of covenantal fidelity and requiring repentance and reconciliation rather than freedom for remarriage.[16] Anthony C. Thiselton highlights that abandonment by a believer constitutes hypocrisy and faithlessness, as it defies the peace and holiness to which Christians are called (1 Cor 7:15), disrupting the covenant's reflection of Christ's love for the *ekklesia* and demanding ecclesiastical discipline.[17] Ben Witherington III notes that Paul sees marriage among believers as a sacred bond under Christ's lordship, where abandonment is a graver sin than by unbelievers because it betrays the faith that should sustain the union, potentially leading to excommunication if unrepented (cf. 1 Cor 5:1-5).[18] Roy E. Ciampa and Brian S. Rosner stress that Paul's distinction between believers and unbelievers in 1 Cor 7:10-16 implies that abandonment by a believer is intolerable, as it undermines the covenantal ethics of the new creation, requiring the church to pursue restoration while recognizing the deep faithlessness involved.[19] These insights collectively affirm that abandonment by a believer is a more severe covenantal violation, as it not only breaks marital trust but also profanes the faith community's witness to divine fidelity, warranting judgment and calling for reconciliation over dissolution.

Scripture explicitly states that God is twice divorced: he divorced Israel, the Northern Kingdom, and Judah, the Southern Kingdom, due to their persistent covenantal unfaithfulness. Judah, despite witnessing Israel's judgment, followed the same path of betrayal, depicted in graphic marital language in Ezek 16 and 23, where both nations are portrayed as unfaithful wives engaging in idolatry and injustice. These divine acts of divorce, grounded in prophetic pronouncements, reflect God's justice in response to covenantal violation, not a mere metaphor but a textual and theological reality.

---

16. Fee, *First Epistle*, 300-302.
17. Thiselton, *First Epistle*, 530-32.
18. Witherington, *Women in the Earliest*, 24-26.
19. Ciampa and Rosner, *First Letter*, 285-87.

THE *EKKLESIA* AS COVENANT FULFILLMENT

With both Israel and Judah cast out, the New Testament introduces the *ekklesia*—the called-out ones—as the bride of Christ (Eph 5:25-27; 2 Cor 11:2; Rev 21:2, 9). This shift does not reflect divine capriciousness but covenantal faithfulness, as God establishes a new covenant through Christ's blood. John Owen emphasizes that God's actions are morally grounded, ensuring that judgment serves righteousness.[20] The *ekklesia* represents a redemptive restoration, affirming the sacredness of covenant despite human failure.

BIBLICAL REALISM ABOUT MARRIAGE

Biblical examples of marriage often depict relational dysfunction more than ideal partnership. Abraham's use of Hagar led to familial strife (Gen 16:4-6); Jacob's polygamous marriages caused rivalry and division (Gen 29:30—30:24); David's adultery with Bathsheba and murder of Uriah violated covenantal fidelity (2 Sam 11:2-27); Solomon's many foreign wives led him into idolatry (1 Kgs 11:1-8); and Hosea's marriage to Gomer symbolized Israel's unfaithfulness yet, God's persistent love (Hos 1:2—3:5). Scripture neither romanticizes nor idealizes marriage but reveals that even divinely chosen individuals struggled with fidelity, love, and covenantal consistency. This realism underscores human insufficiency to maintain covenant and the centrality of divine grace, as seen in Jesus' teaching, which balances the Edenic ideal with human frailty:

> "Because of your hardness of heart Moses permitted you to divorce your wives; but from the beginning it has not been this way." (Matt 19:8)

TOWARD A COVENANTAL THEOLOGY OF DIVORCE

Through a renewed understanding of divine faithfulness, prophetic justice, and ecclesial grace, Christians may recover a covenantally grounded vision of marriage that is both holy and honest. Divine faithfulness,

---

20. Owen, *Works of John Owen*, 234-35.

seen in God's commitment despite Israel's betrayal—"I will allure her, bring her into the wilderness and speak kindly to her" (Hos 2:14-20)—sets the standard for covenant.

Prophetic justice, as in God's divorce of Israel and Judah, upholds the moral necessity of addressing betrayal.[21] Ecclesial grace, embodied in the *ekklesia*, points to redemption, as Jürgen Moltmann describes in the tension between the "already" of Christ's victory and the "not yet" of eschatological fulfillment.[22] This vision neither trivializes marriage's sacredness nor condemns those facing covenantal breakdown but reflects the divine pattern of covenant, judgment, and grace.

CONCLUSION

The continual biblical allusions to faithlessness suggest that we may be able to learn as much about covenant fidelity from its successes as we can from its failures; this is especially true for the *ekklesia*. The covenant describes a relationship and its terms; it is essentially an agreement. What it can't do is live the relationship and experience the dynamics that are a fundamental part of every relationship. It cannot express the joys or the sorrows, or the anticipation that foments the intimacy of two becoming one. So it should come as no surprise that the Bible's narratives don't attempt to sanitize the dynamics of marriage and hide the messiness of divorce; rather they present the best and worst of what is possible both in and apart from covenant faithfulness.

---

21. Wenham, *Book of Leviticus*, 250-52.
22. Moltmann, *Theology of Hope*, 224-25.

7

The Ineradicable Holiness of the Seventh-Day Sabbath

Holiness as Set Apart and Purposeful

INTRODUCTION: REDISCOVERING THE PURPOSEFUL HOLINESS OF THE SABBATH

ACROSS CENTURIES OF THEOLOGICAL development, the Sabbath has often been treated as either a Jewish relic or a flexible moral symbol. Rarely has serious consideration been given to the ontological grounding of the Sabbath's holiness in the very nature of God. Holiness in the biblical sense is not static separation but purposeful sanctification.[1] This chapter asserts that the seventh-day Sabbath remains and is holy not by human observance, but because God has both set it apart and infused it with purpose—namely, cessation from labor. It is by definition an extension of the very nature of God. This pause is neither ceremonial nor temporary, but central to God's identity, creation order, redemptive plan, and eschatological hope, as articulated by theologians like Samuele Bacchiocchi and Sigve K. Tonstad.[2]

---

1. Brown et al., *Hebrew and English Lexicon*, 1964–76.
2. Bacchiocchi, *Divine Rest*, 45–50; Tonstad, *Lost Meaning*, 12–15.

HOLINESS IN SCRIPTURE: SET APART AND PURPOSEFUL

In both Hebrew (*qāḏaš*) and Greek (*hagiazō*), the verb "to sanctify" involves designating something for divine use.[3] Holiness is often misinterpreted as mere otherness or inaccessibility. However, a biblical-theological survey reveals that holiness is deeply tied to divine function: the temple is holy because it is where God meets his people (Exod 29:43), the priest is holy because he mediates that presence (Lev 21:8), and the Sabbath is holy because it is a sanctuary in time—where rest, joy, and communion with the Creator take place (Gen 2:3). Abraham Joshua Heschel describes the Sabbath as a "palace in time," reflecting its divine purpose.[4] Richard M. Davidson emphasizes that the Sabbath's holiness reflects God's character, serving as a covenantal sign of divine-human relationship.[5] Because God is holy, only he can make holy, and his holiness—being an attribute of his nature—cannot be unmade.

THE SABBATH AS A CREATION ORDINANCE: PAST, PRESENT, AND FUTURE

Genesis 2:1–3 introduces the Sabbath as a climax to creation:

> Then God blessed the seventh day and sanctified it, because on it He rested from all His work which God had created and made. (2:3)

Unlike the other six days, the seventh day lacks the closing formula "evening and morning," suggesting its open-ended, eschatological character and its infused nature (Gen 2:3). Exodus 20:11 ties the Decalogue's Sabbath command to creation and Sinai:

> "I am the Lord your God, who brought you out of the land of Egypt, out of the house of slavery. . . . For in six days the Lord made the heavens and the earth . . . and He rested on the seventh day; for that reason the Lord blessed the Sabbath day and made it holy." (Exod 20:2, 11)

---

3. For "qāḏaš," see Brown et al., *Hebrew and English Lexicon*, 871–72; for "hagiazō," see Kittel and Friedrich, *Theological Dictionary*, 88–115.
4. Heschel, *Sabbath*, 10–12.
5. Davidson, *Love of God*, 32–34.

This dual emphasis amplifies God's holiness by linking redemption and creation.[6] The Sabbath is thus tri-directional: it remembers God's completed creation (past), links weekly rest to redemption (present), and anticipates the eschatological rest in Christ, encompassing both the present and the future, as confirmed by Heb 4:9–11: "So there remains a Sabbath rest for the people of God" (v. 9). Sigve K. Tonstad underscores this eschatological dimension, arguing that the Sabbath points to God's ultimate rest in the new creation.[7]

CHRIST AND THE FULFILLMENT OF SABBATH PURPOSE

Jesus neither nullified nor replaced the Sabbath. He affirmed it through action and word. Luke 4:16 states it was his "custom" to attend synagogue on the Sabbath. In Mark 2:27–28, he declares,

> "The Sabbath was made for man, and not man for the Sabbath. So the Son of Man is Lord even of the Sabbath."

Jesus' teaching and healing on the Sabbath were restorative, not abolitionist, aligning with its purpose of human flourishing. In Matt 11:28–30, his invitation to find rest in him draws directly on the Sabbath theology of liberation and redemption: "Come to Me, all who are weary... and I will give you rest" (v. 28). Hebrews 4:9 affirms an enduring *sabbatismos* for God's people, fulfilled in Christ yet tied to the seventh day. Jesus' affirmation of the Sabbath vis-à-vis his actions affirm its holy nature.[8]

RESPONDING TO SCRIPTURAL AND THEOLOGICAL OBJECTIONS

Objection 1: Colossians 2:16–17 is often cited to argue that the Sabbath was a shadow now obsolete in Christ:

> Therefore, no one is to act as your judge in regard to food and drink, or in respect to a festival or a new moon, or a Sabbath

---

6. Levenson, *Creation and the Persistence*, 100–102.
7. Tonstad, *Lost Meaning*, 120–25.
8. White, *The Desire of Ages*, 206–7.

day—things which are only a shadow of what is to come; but the substance belongs to Christ.

However, the text refers to ceremonial sabbaths (Lev 23:1–44), not the seventh-day Sabbath. The triad "festival, new moon, sabbath" reflects ceremonial cycles (cf. Hos 2:11), not creation ordinances.[9] Samuele Bacchiocchi clarifies that Colossians addresses Jewish ceremonial laws, not the moral Sabbath of the Decalogue.[10]

Objection 2: Romans 14:5–6 speaks of personal convictions about days: "One person regards one day above another, another regards every day alike" (v. 5). The context is asceticism and dietary practices, not moral law. Paul does not suggest that the Sabbath, a Ten Commandments institution, is optional.[11]

Objection 3: Galatians 4:9–10 refers to turning back to "weak and worthless elemental things" (v. 9). Paul's concern is with legalism and calendar rituals for justification, not creation-based commandments. Richard M. Davidson argues that the Sabbath's moral grounding distinguishes it from such rituals.[12] Paul affirms that "the Law is holy, and the commandment is holy and righteous and good" (Rom 7:12).

Objection 4: The New Testament lacks a specific re-commandment of the Sabbath. Yet, Jesus (Luke 4:16), Paul (Acts 13:14, 42, 44), and others observed the Sabbath regularly. In Mark 2:28, Jesus declared himself Lord of the Sabbath. The clear implication, given the context, has to do with his authority, which no man, council, or earthly power can abrogate. Hebrews 4:9 affirms an enduring Sabbath rest (*sabbatismos*) for the people of God.

Objection 5: Some argue Jesus fulfilled the law and thus nullified the Sabbath. Yet, fulfillment in Matt 5:17 means to establish and elevate:

> "Do not presume that I came to abolish the Law or the Prophets; I did not come to abolish, but to fulfill."

Isaiah 42:21 foretells the Messiah would "magnify the law and make it honorable."

---

9. Bacchiocchi, *From Sabbath to Sunday*, 55–60.
10. Bacchiocchi, *From Sabbath to Sunday*, 58–62.
11. Davidson, *Love of God*, 35–36.
12. Davidson, *Love of God*, 35–36.

Objection 6: The Sabbath is allegedly Mosaic, not moral. However, Gen 2:3 shows it was instituted at creation. Exodus 20:11 confirms its moral grounding, predating Israel and is thus universal.

Objection 7: Early church practice allegedly shifted to Sunday. While post-apostolic documents reference Sunday gatherings, the Bible never declares Sunday holy and there are no explicit or implicit commands or exhortations indicating the diminution of the Sabbath or the exaltation of the first day of the week. Descriptive acts do not overturn prescriptive commands.[13] Samuele Bacchiocchi's historical analysis shows that Sunday observance emerged later, lacking biblical warrant.[14]

THEOLOGICAL IMPLICATIONS AND FINAL REFLECTION

The Sabbath is infused with God's holiness and is a perpetual sign of God's covenant faithfulness. To discard it is to impinge on God's nature and to attempt to erase a sacred marker in time that reveals God's holiness—a Creator who ceased from creating, a Redeemer who restores, and a King who reigns. The Sabbath is not merely a shadow to be dismissed; it is a light to be more fully entered through Christ. Its holiness, grounded in God's own holiness, i.e., set apart and purposeful, cannot be undone by tradition or silence. It is a gift, an invitation, a rhythm, not simply an ordinance but a revelation of divine intention. Walter Brueggemann emphasizes the Sabbath as a countercultural act of resistance against human striving, reflecting God's restful sovereignty.[15]

---

13. Pelikan, *Christian Tradition*, 120–25.
14. Bacchiocchi, *From Sabbath to Sunday*, 65–70.
15. Brueggemann, *Sabbath as Resistance*, 20–25.

8

Is the Bible the Word of God?

THE QUESTION OF WHETHER the Bible is the word of God is a cornerstone of Christian theology, like a foundation stone tested by storms of doubt and inquiry. It sparks rigorous debate, with two primary perspectives: (1) the Bible does not explicitly call itself the word of God, with Jesus Christ identified as the true Word (Logos) in the New Testament, and (2) the Bible is the divinely inspired written word of God. These reflect competing worldviews: a materialist perspective demanding empirical proof and a spiritual perspective grounded in faith. This chapter argues that belief in the Bible as the word of God is a faith proposition, robustly supported by logical arguments from key New Testament texts—1 Thess 2:13, 1 Cor 14:37, and Rev 1:1–3—alongside other biblical references and believers' transformative experiences. It also examines the historical rise of the materialist perspective during the Enlightenment and its development through German scholarship.

THE MATERIALIST PERSPECTIVE: THE BIBLE AS A HUMAN CONSTRUCT

The materialist perspective, rooted in critical scholarship, views the Bible as a human artifact shaped by cultural and theological contexts, not unequivocally the word of God. It prioritizes empirical evidence and textual analysis.

Key Arguments of the Materialist Perspective

1. **Textual and manuscript evidence:** The Bible's transmission reveals complexities. The Hebrew Bible exists in multiple traditions (Masoretic Text, Septuagint, Dead Sea Scrolls) with textual variants. The New Testament's 5,700-plus Greek manuscripts contain thousands of variants, raising questions about reliability.[1] Without original autographs, claims of divine authorship face scrutiny.

2. **Formation of the canon:** The canonization process involved human decisions. The Hebrew Bible's canon was finalized around 90 CE at Jamnia, and the New Testament canon emerged through fourth-century debates.[2] Lee Martin McDonald argues that these were theological and political processes, not clearly divinely mandated.[3]

3. **Christological distinction:** John 1:1–14 identifies Jesus as the Logos, suggesting the Bible, as a text, is distinct from the divine Word.

4. **Deconstruction of inspiration:** The term *theopneustos* ("God-breathed") in 2 Tim 3:16 is ambiguous, possibly referring to Old Testament texts or early Christian writings, reflecting human experiences rather than direct divine authorship.[4]

Historical Background of the Materialist Perspective

The Enlightenment (seventeenth to eighteenth century) elevated reason and skepticism, shaping the materialist perspective. Baruch Spinoza's *Tractatus Theologico-Politicus* (1670) treated the Bible as a historical document subject to human influences.[5] German scholarship in the

---

1. Ehrman, *Misquoting Jesus*, 10–11.
2. Eusebius, *Church History*, 125–27.
3. McDonald, *Biblical Canon*, 38–40.
4. Achtemeier, *Inspiration and Authority*, 45–47.
5. Spinoza, *Tractatus Theologico-Politicus*, 12–15.

nineteenth century, particularly the Tübingen School, advanced this perspective:

- Karl Barth (1886–1968) argued the Bible becomes God's word through divine encounter, not as an inherently divine text.[6]
- Rudolf Bultmann (1884–1976) used form criticism, viewing the Bible as a human document expressing existential truths.[7]
- Emil Brunner (1889–1966) saw the Bible as a human witness to Christ, prioritizing encounter over inerrancy.[8]

These scholars emphasized human agency, challenging divine inspiration claims.

THE SPIRITUAL PERSPECTIVE: THE BIBLE AS THE WORD OF GOD

The spiritual perspective, articulated by J. I. Packer and Wayne Grudem, asserts the Bible's divine inspiration, supported by textual evidence and transformative impact, requires faith.

Key Arguments of the Spiritual Perspective

1. **Biblical self-attestation:** Old Testament prophets used "Thus says the Lord" over 3,800 times (e.g., Isa 1:2). Second Timothy 3:16 and 2 Pet 1:21 describe Scripture as God-breathed and Spirit-guided.
2. **Thematic unity:** The Bible's coherence across 1,500 years, with themes like redemption (Isa 53; Matt 8:17), suggests divine oversight.[9]
3. **Transformative power:** Hebrews 4:12 calls the word "living and active," shaping lives through spiritual renewal.[10]

---

6. Barth, *Church Dogmatics*, 1/2, 509–10.
7. Bultmann, *Theology*, 20–22.
8. Brunner, *Christian Doctrine*, 110–12.
9. Bruce, *Canon of Scripture*, 255–57.
10. Wright, *Case for the Psalms*, 25–27.

4. **Faith-based epistemology:** Hebrews 11:1 defines faith as "the assurance of things hoped for," underpinning belief in the Bible's authority (John 20:29).

Logical Arguments from Key Texts

1 Thess 2:13:

> For this reason we also thank God continually that when you received the word of God, which you heard from us, you accepted it not as the word of mere men, but as what it truly is, the word of God, which also is at work in you who believe.

Paul's oral proclamation is recognized as divine, with its transformative power tied to faith. This extends to written epistles (2 Pet 3:16), supporting a faith-based acceptance. Gordon D. Fee notes the early church's view of apostolic preaching as divinely authoritative.[11]

1 Cor 14:37:

> If anyone thinks he is a prophet or spiritual, let him recognize that the things which I write to you are the Lord's command.

Paul's writings are divine commands (*entolē*), akin to Jesus' words (John 12:49–50), recognized as scripture (2 Pet 3:16). Anthony C. Thiselton highlights Paul's apostolic authority.[12]

Rev 1:1–3:

> The Revelation of Jesus Christ, which God gave Him . . . communicated it by His angel to His bond-servant John, who testified to the word of God and to the testimony of Jesus Christ.

The explicit divine origin extends to other apostolic writings (2 Pet 1:21). G. K. Beale compares this to Old Testament prophetic claims (Jer 1:2).[13]

---

11. Fee, *First and Second Letters*, 84–86.
12. Thiselton, *First Epistle*, 1132–34.
13. Beale, *Book of Revelation*, 181–83.

Ethical Appeal

God's choice of humble authors—fishermen, tax collectors—over scholars or rulers underscores divine intent to communicate through accessible voices (Matt 4:18–22; Luke 5:27–28).

THE FAITH PROPOSITION: OLD AND NEW TESTAMENT EVIDENCE

Belief in the Bible as God's word is a faith proposition, supported by textual and experiential evidence. Old Testament prophets claimed divine authority (Amos 1:3; Ezek 2:4), with Deut 4:2 and Ps 119:105 affirming Scripture's sacredness. New Testament texts affirm Old Testament authority (Matt 5:17) and claim inspiration (John 12:49–50; 2 Pet 3:16). The Sermon on the Mount (Matt 5–7) and Rom 8:28–39 guide believers ethically and existentially through faith.

THE BIBLE AS THE WORD OF GOD: A TRANSFORMATIVE INSTRUMENT

Encounter, the expression of existential truths, and a human witness to Christ notwithstanding, absent a clear definition of the word of God, these ideas risk blending into an indistinct amalgam. This section proposes that the Bible is instrumental, a divinely inspired document penned by human authors, possessing utility to effect transformation through the illumination of the Holy Spirit. Emphasizing its materiality obscures its instrumentality as a means of spiritual transformation. The Bible is not merely the word from God or about God but the word invested by God, encompassing objective, subjective, intersubjective, and intrasubjective dimensions, unified in a singular, transformative expression.[14]

The objective mode views the Bible as divine revelation, historically and textually grounded, as in 2 Tim 3:16: "All Scripture is inspired by God and profitable for teaching." The subjective mode emphasizes personal interpretation and emotional response, as in Prov 3:5: "Trust in the Lord with all your heart." The intersubjective mode reflects communal

---

14. 2 Tim 3:16.

interpretation within the *ekklesia*, as seen in Acts 2:42, where believers "devoted themselves to the apostles' teaching." These modes complement the intrasubjective, which internalizes Scripture's transformative power, shaping the believer's inner life.[15] Intrasubjective, defined as the internalized, Spirit-mediated experience of Scripture that reshapes consciousness and volition, highlights how the word operates within the believer's soul, not merely as external revelation or communal doctrine.[16] This "spiritually metabolized" process, where Scripture is integrated into the believer's moral and existential framework through the Holy Spirit, distinguishes the intrasubjective mode.[17]

KEY DIMENSIONS OF INTRASUBJECTIVE APPLICATION

1. **Spiritual integration**

   The word becomes part of one's moral compass, emotional landscape, and existential framework. Psalm 119:11 illustrates this: "I have hidden your word in my heart that I might not sin against you." James K. A. Smith argues that Scripture shapes the believer's affections and imagination, aligning with this intrasubjective integration.[18]

2. **Dialogical interior life**

   The believer engages in an inner conversation with God through Scripture, echoing Augustine's *Confessions*, where Scripture is not just read but heard inwardly as a divine voice.[19] This dialogue fosters a dynamic relationship with God's word.

3. **Transformative renewal**

   Romans 12:2 speaks of being "transformed by the renewing of your mind," an intrasubjective process where the word reshapes cognition and volition. Kevin J. Vanhoozer describes this as Scripture's

---

15. Prov 3:5; Acts 2:42; Ps 119:11.
16. Acts 2:42.
17. Ps 119:11.
18. Smith, *Desiring the Kingdom*, 65–67.
19. See Augustine, *Confessions*, 10.3.3 (224).

performative role, transforming believers into participants in God's redemptive drama.[20]

4. **Conviction and consolation**

   The word convicts (Heb 4:12) and consoles (Ps 23), not as external truths but as felt realities within the soul's depths.

5. **Mystical union**

   In contemplative Christian traditions, the word is experienced as Christ's living presence, as in John 15:7: "If you abide in me and my words abide in you...." John Webster notes that this union reflects Scripture's role in fostering covenantal intimacy with Christ.[21]

THEOLOGICAL IMPLICATION

To say the Bible is the word of God intrasubjectively is to affirm that it is not merely spoken to us but spoken within us, becoming a living voice in the conscience, a lamp to the inner path, and a mirror of the soul. This dimension is crucial for covenantal theology, where divine speech is embodied in the believer, shaping their identity as part of Christ's *ekklesia* and fostering a lived theology of faithfulness. The intrasubjective mode enables believers to internalize the covenant, aligning their lives with God's redemptive purposes, as seen in the transformative witness of the early church (Acts 2:42–47).

COVENANTAL PROGRESSION: FROM SHADOW TO REALITY IN GOD'S WORD

David understood the Torah as the word of God, as evident in Ps 119:89—"Forever, Lord, Your word stands in heaven"—viewing it as divine speech guiding covenantal life.[22] John Goldingay notes that David's view reflects the Torah's authoritative role in shaping Israel's covenantal identity. The Torah is the old covenant, embodying the Mosaic agreement between God and Israel (Exod 24:7; Deut 29:1). Gordon Wenham

---

20. Vanhoozer, *Drama of Doctrine*, 159–61.
21. John Webster, *Holy Scripture*, 92–94.
22. Goldingay, *Psalms*, 346–48.

explains that the Torah encapsulates the covenant's terms, binding Israel to God through law and promise.[23] The new covenant has been in force since the cross, inaugurated by Christ's blood (Luke 22:20; Heb 9:15), making it the word of God as the fulfillment of divine promise. F. F. Bruce argues that Christ's death enacts the new covenant, establishing it as God's living word of grace.[24] The old covenant was the shadow, prefiguring the good things to come (Heb 10:1; Col 2:17), while the new covenant is the reality, realized in Christ. N. T. Wright posits that the old covenant's laws prefigure the new covenant's embodied grace in Christ.[25] Christ is the author of the new covenant, written on the hearts of the covenant community (Heb 12:2; Jer 31:33; Heb 8:10), mediating a direct, internalized relationship with God. Karl Barth describes Christ as the covenant's originator, inscribing it on hearts through the Spirit.[26] Therefore, the Bible is the word of God inscribed, the written testimony of divine revelation (2 Tim 3:16), and Jesus is the Word made flesh, the incarnate reality (John 1:14). Kevin Vanhoozer views the Bible as the "inscripturated Word," testifying to Christ the incarnate Word, uniting divine revelation in covenantal purpose.[27]

ADDRESSING COUNTERARGUMENTS

Materialists may argue that the Bible's authority lies solely in its objective text, dismissing the intrasubjective as subjective mysticism. However, this overlooks the Holy Spirit's role in transforming believers intrasubjectively, as affirmed in Rom 12:2, where renewal is a divine act.[28] Craig Bartholomew counters that Scripture's authority encompasses both its objective truth and its transformative power, mediated by the Spirit within the community of faith. This holistic view unifies the epistemic modes, challenging materialist reductions and affirming the Bible's instrumentality.

---

23. Wenham, *Exploring the Old Testament*, 134–36.
24. Bruce, *Epistle to the Hebrews*, 216–18.
25. Wright, *New Testament*, 403–5.
26. Barth, *Church Dogmatics*, 4/1, 304–6.
27. Vanhoozer, *Drama of Doctrine*, 155–57.
28. Bartholomew, *Introducing Biblical Hermeneutics*, 45–47.

Comparison of Epistemic Modes of the Word

Mode	Description	Example Passage
Objective	The word as divine revelation, historically and textually	2 Tim 3:16
Subjective	Personal interpretation or emotional response	Prov 3:5
Intersubjective	Shared theological understanding within community	Acts 2:42
Intrasubjective	Internalized, spiritually transformative experience	Ps 119:11

Table 1

CONCLUSIONS

Materialist and Spiritual Tensions

The debate over whether the Bible is the word of God reflects a fundamental tension between materialist and spiritual worldviews. The materialist perspective, rooted in Enlightenment rationalism and advanced by scholars like Barth, Bultmann, and Brunner, views the Bible as a human artifact shaped by cultural and historical contexts, emphasizing textual variants and human canonization processes. In contrast, the spiritual perspective, articulated by Packer, Grudem, and others, affirms the Bible's divine inspiration through its self-attestation, thematic unity, and transformative power, supported by texts like 1 Thess 2:13, 1 Cor 14:37, and Rev 1:1–3. This perspective prioritizes faith as the lens for recognizing the Bible's authority, rejecting materialist demands for empirical proof as misaligned with spiritual realities.[29]

The Bible's Transformative Instrumentality

The Bible's role as a transformative instrument transcends materialist critiques by integrating objective, subjective, intersubjective, and intrasubjective dimensions into a unified expression of God's word. The intrasubjective mode, where Scripture is internalized through the Holy Spirit, reshapes believers' moral and existential frameworks, as seen in

---

29. Smith, *Desiring the Kingdom*, 65–67; Vanhoozer, *Drama of Doctrine*, 159–61.

Ps 119:11 and Rom 12:2.[30] Scholars like Smith and Vanhoozer affirm that this internalization fosters a lived theology, where the word becomes a dynamic presence within the believer's soul, guiding conscience and fostering covenantal intimacy. This transformative power counters materialist reductions, affirming the Bible's divine origin through its impact on lives.

Covenantal Progression and Christ as the Word

The Bible's identity as the word of God is rooted in its covenantal progression from the old to the new covenant, unifying its role as divine revelation.[31] David's view of the Torah as God's word (Ps 119:89) and its embodiment of the old covenant (Exod 24:7) establish its divine authority, while the new covenant, inaugurated at the cross (Luke 22:20), fulfills this as the reality in Christ (Heb 10:1). Christ, as the author of the new covenant written on believers' hearts (Jer 31:33), is the Word made flesh (John 1:14), with the Bible as the inscripturated testimony. This progression, as Wright and Barth note, integrates the epistemic modes, with the intrasubjective mode reflecting the new covenant's internalization in the *ekklesia*.

Implications for Faith and Practice

Belief in the Bible as God's word is a faith proposition, robustly supported by its self-attestation, coherence, and transformative impact. The spiritual perspective invites believers to approach Scripture with faith, as Heb 11:1 encourages, trusting its divine inspiration to guide ethical and existential living (Matt 5–7; Rom 8:28–39). By embracing the Bible's instrumentality, the *ekklesia* embodies the new covenant, fostering a community where the word shapes hearts and lives, countering materialist skepticism with a lived witness to Christ's reality. This holistic understanding calls Christians to engage Scripture not as a static text but as a living, Spirit-mediated word, transforming individuals and communities in covenantal faithfulness.

---

30. Wright, *New Testament*, 403–5; Barth, *Church Dogmatics*, 1/1, 304–6.
31. Webster, *Holy Scripture*, 92–94; Acts 2:42–47.

9

A Theology and Philosophy of the Soul
A Conditionalist Perspective

THE NATURE OF THE soul has been a subject of intense debate within Christian theology for centuries. Traditional perspectives, often shaped by Platonism and Hellenistic dualism, depict the soul as an immaterial, inherently immortal entity distinct from the body. In contrast, this chapter articulates a conditionalist perspective, defining the soul as the nonmaterial sum total of a person's human experience, uniquely distinguished as a *soul-print* and attached to the life of God, conditionally immortal through divine sustenance. This chapter defends this view with scriptural and theological support, responds to common objections, and explores its implications for Christian theology and practice.

THE SOUL DEFINED: A CONDITIONALIST FRAMEWORK

In this conditionalist framework, the soul is the immaterial and unique human experience that distinguishes one individual from another, herein described as a "soul-print." This soul-print encapsulates the distinct personal imprint of an individual's life experience, akin to a fingerprint that uniquely identifies each person who has ever lived. It is neither the divine breath nor the physical body, nor merely a combination of both, but the singular narrative of one's existence. The life of the individual is derived from God's life, and their life experience results in this unique soul-print, which may cease to exist following divine judgment or continue in God's life. Genesis 2:7 uses the Hebrew term *nephesh ḥayyah*, best translated as "living person" rather than "immortal soul," stating,

> Then the Lord God formed the man of dust from the ground, and breathed into his nostrils the breath of life; and the man became a living person.

SCRIPTURAL AND HISTORICAL SUPPORT

Scripture consistently frames the soul as a relational entity contingent on God's sustaining power. Genesis 2:7 describes humanity becoming a *nephesh ḥayyah*—a living being—through God's breath, not receiving a soul as a separate entity. Psalm 146:4 and Eccl 12:7 affirm that the body returns to dust and the breath to God, without suggesting continued consciousness. In the New Testament, Luke 20:38 declares, "Now He is not the God of the dead, but of the living; for all live to Him," indicating that the soul-print persists only through relationship with God. John 11:25–26 reinforces this, with Jesus stating, "I am the resurrection and the life; he who believes in Me will live even if he dies," tying eternal life to faith in Christ rather than an innate quality of the soul.

Historically, early Christian thinkers like Irenaeus and Tertullian supported conditional immortality. Irenaeus, in *Against Heresies*, argued that the soul depends on God for life, rejecting inherent immortality as a pagan notion.[1] Tertullian, in *De Anima*, described the soul as material and mortal, contingent on divine judgment.[2] Gregory of Nyssa, while affirming the soul's capacity for immortality, tied this potential to union with God, aligning with the conditionalist view.[3] Plato, whose philosophy influenced early Christian thought, described the soul as the principle of life and individuality, a concept that resonates with the soul-print as the unique imprint of human experience, though Plato's view of inherent continued immortality is rejected here in favor of continued

---

1. Irenaeus, *Against Heresies*, 412–13.
2. Tertullian, *De Anima*, 187–88.
3. Gregory of Nyssa, *On the Soul*, 439–40.

divine dependence.⁴ Aristotle's concept of the soul as the form of the body further supports the soul-print as the immaterial configuration of human experience, dependent on divine sustenance.⁵ Contemporary theologians like N. T. Wright and Nancey Murphy advocate a holistic anthropology, rejecting disembodied immortality in favor of resurrection-based identity.⁶ John Polkinghorne and Peter van Inwagen further support divine reassembly, where God preserves the soul's identity—its soul-print—without requiring continuous consciousness.⁷

1. Human Life Derives from God

The idea that all human life originates in God is foundational to Christian anthropology:

- Genesis 2:7: "Then the Lord God formed the man of dust from the ground, and breathed into his nostrils the breath of life; and the man became a living person." This breath (Hebrew *ruach*) is not merely oxygen—it is divine animation. The soul-print is not self-originating; it is a gift from God.⁸

- Acts 17:28: "For in Him we live and move and exist." Paul affirms that our very existence, including our unique soul-print, is sustained by God, suggesting that our lives are embedded in divine reality.

2. The Soul as Nonmaterial and Enduring

The concept that only the nonmaterial can endure in a world subject to entropy aligns with biblical descriptions of the soul's permanence:

- Ecclesiastes 12:7: "Then the dust will return to the earth as it was, and the spirit will return to God who gave it." The body decays, but

---

4. Plato, *Phaedo*, 78b–84b.
5. Aristotle, *De Anima*, bk. 2, ch. 1, 412a–b.
6. Wright, *Surprised by Hope*, 139–42; Murphy and Green, *Whatever Happened*, 17–29.
7. Polkinghorne, *God of Hope*, 101–4; van Inwagen, "Possibility of Resurrection," 145–49.
8. Brown et al., *Hebrew and English Lexicon*, 1906.

the soul-print returns to its source—God—affirming its sustainability beyond physical entropy.

- Matthew 10:28: "Do not be afraid of those who kill the body but are unable to kill the soul; but rather fear Him who is able to destroy both soul and body in hell." Jesus distinguishes between the destructible body and the indestructible soul-print, reinforcing its transcendence of material decay.

3. Entropy and the Curse of Sin

The concept of entropy—disorder and decay—mirrors the biblical curse on creation due to sin:

- Romans 8:20–21: "For the creation was subjected to futility . . . in hope that the creation itself also will be set free from its slavery to corruption." Paul describes a cosmic entropy, with the soul-print preserved in God's life beyond this decay.[9]
- Hebrews 1:10–12: "They will perish, but You remain; And they all will wear out like a garment" (v. 11). This poetic imagery of the universe wearing out echoes the second law of thermodynamics and affirms the theological framing of the soul-print's endurance.

4. The Soul-Print: Experience Preserved in God

The metaphor of a soul-print suggests that our lived experience leaves a lasting, unique impression on God's life, distinguishing each individual as a fingerprint distinguishes one person from another. This aligns with biblical ideas of divine remembrance and personal identity:

- Psalm 139:16: "Your eyes have seen my formless substance; / And in Your book were written / All the days that were ordained for me, / When as yet there was not one of them." God's memory actively preserves the soul-print of each life.
- Malachi 3:16: "Then those who feared the Lord spoke to one another, and the Lord listened attentively and heard it, and a book of

---

9. Polkinghorne, *God of Hope*, 98–100.

remembrance was written before Him for those who fear the Lord and esteem His name." This scroll metaphor supports the idea that each soul-print is recorded in God's consciousness.

5. Resurrection as Divine Continuity

If the soul-print is preserved in God, then resurrection becomes not just possible but inevitable:

- John 11:25: "I am the resurrection and the life; the one who believes in Me will live, even if he dies." Jesus links resurrection to divine life itself—what is preserved as a soul-print in God cannot remain dead.
- 1 Corinthians 15:42–44: "So also is the resurrection of the dead. It is sown a perishable body, it is raised an imperishable body; . . . it is sown a natural body, it is raised a spiritual body." Resurrection transforms the soul-print into spiritual permanence.

Theological Reflection

The metaphor of the soul-print offers a rich synthesis of biblical anthropology, metaphysics, and eschatology. It suggests that:

- Each life uniquely reflects God's image (*imago Dei*), embodied in its distinct soul-print.
- The soul, as a nonmaterial soul-print, resists entropy and is preserved in divine memory.
- Resurrection is not a reversal of death but a fulfillment of divine continuity for each soul-print.

This concept draws from Plato's notion of the soul as the essence of individual identity, though reoriented within a conditionalist framework to emphasize divine dependence over inherent immortality.[10] It is a poetic and philosophically robust way to affirm that no life is lost in God and

---

10. Plato, *Phaedo*, 78b–84b.

that resurrection is a divine necessity, aligning with Oscar Cullmann's emphasis on resurrection over immortality.[11]

RESPONSES TO CHALLENGES

Several objections arise against the conditionalist view of the soul, each addressed to maintain theological coherence:

1. Moral continuity and postmortem identity: Critics argue that if the soul perishes, moral continuity and postmortem identity are undermined, complicating divine justice. This view responds that the soul-print, as the sum of human experience, persists in the divine life until final judgment, as implied by Rev 20:14–15, where the "second death" follows judgment. This ensures moral accountability without requiring continued immortality, as God preserves the soul-print for justice's sake.

2. Distinction between soul and consciousness: Some challenge the separation of the soul as human experience from personal consciousness. This framework clarifies that the soul-print, as unique identity, is stored in God's life without retaining individual consciousness, a concept supported by theologians like Polkinghorne and van Inwagen.[12] This divine preservation maintains the soul-print's integrity without necessitating continuous awareness.

3. Biblical texts on destruction: Matthew 10:28 states, "Do not fear those who kill the body but are unable to kill the soul; but rather fear Him who is able to destroy both soul and body in hell," explicitly supporting the soul-print's conditional nature, as only God can destroy it. Critics citing Luke 16:19–31 (the parable of the rich man and Lazarus) to argue for continued postmortem existence are countered by recognizing the text as a parable, not a metaphysical treatise.

---

11. Cullmann, *Immortality of the Soul*, 48–50.

12. Polkinghorne, *God of Hope*, 103–4; van Inwagen, "Possibility of Resurrection," 147–48.

A THEOLOGY AND PHILOSOPHY OF THE SOUL

COMPARATIVE ANALYSIS WITH CONTEMPORARY PERSPECTIVES

To further illuminate the conditionalist perspective presented here, it is instructive to compare it with the views of two contemporary thinkers: Richard Swinburne, who advocates a nonmaterialist, substance dualist approach, and Luke Janssen, who represents a materialist viewpoint. Each author's position is outlined below, followed by a comparison to the conditionalist framework of the soul as a nonmaterial soul-print conditionally immortal through divine sustenance.

Richard Swinburne's nonmaterialist perspective posits the soul as an immaterial, purely mental substance distinct from the body, essential for personal identity, consciousness, and moral responsibility. In *The Evolution of the Soul* and *Are We Bodies or Souls?*, Swinburne argues that humans are composite beings of body and soul, with the soul as the core self that persists beyond death. He defends substance dualism, asserting that mental phenomena like qualia and free will cannot be reduced to physical processes, and that the soul interacts with the brain while remaining ontologically independent, ensuring the possibility of an afterlife.[13]

In comparison to the conditionalist view, Swinburne's emphasis on the soul as an immaterial substance aligns with the nonmaterial nature of the soul-print, rejecting purely physical explanations for human identity. However, the conditionalist framework diverges by rejecting inherent immortality, positing the soul-print's endurance as contingent on divine sustenance rather than an essential property of the soul itself. While Swinburne sees the soul as naturally persisting, the conditionalist perspective stresses divine dependence, avoiding Platonic influences and emphasizing resurrection as the means of continuity, thus maintaining the nuances of biblical relational ontology without altering the novel conditionalist nuances.

Luke Janssen's materialist approach views the soul not as an immaterial entity but as an emergent property of the brain and body, reconcilable with neuroscience and biblical anthropology. In works like *Soul-Searching: The Evolution of Judeo-Christian Thinking on the Soul and the Afterlife* and presentations such as "The Human Soul: Immaterial Substance or Emergent Property of the Brain?" Janssen argues that

---

13. Swinburne, *Evolution of the Soul*, 154–78; Swinburne, *Are We Bodies*, 45–67.

biblical terms like *nephesh* and *psyche* denote the whole living person rather than a disembodied spirit. He posits that consciousness arises from neural activity, and immortality involves God's re-creation of the physical person, rejecting dualism for a holistic, embodied identity grounded in science and theology.[14]

Compared to the conditionalist perspective, Janssen's materialism contrasts sharply by denying any nonmaterial soul, whereas the soul-print is explicitly nonmaterial, encapsulating human experience preserved in God's life. The conditionalist view shares Janssen's emphasis on divine re-creation for resurrection but maintains the soul-print's immaterial uniqueness, distinguishing it from emergent physical properties. This preserves the conditionalist nuances of divine sustenance and conditional immortality, integrating biblical holism without reducing the soul to materiality, thus highlighting a middle ground that affirms nonmaterial experience while rejecting inherent dualistic immortality.

BROADER IMPLICATIONS AND REDEFINING "SOUL"

This conditionalist perspective challenges inherited assumptions about the soul by rejecting Hellenistic dualism and embracing a biblical, relational ontology. The soul, as a soul-print, is not a ghostly residue but the immaterial configuration of human experience, uniquely preserved in the divine life. This view aligns with N. T. Wright's emphasis on resurrection over disembodied immortality, arguing that Christian hope lies in bodily resurrection.[15] Nancey Murphy's non-reductive physicalism further supports this, emphasizing identity through divine action rather than an independent soul.[16]

Practically, this theology shapes Christian living in the following ways:

- Relational identity: Believers cultivate their soul-print through relationship with God, fostering spiritual disciplines like prayer and worship (Ps 42:1–2).

---

14. Janssen, *Soul-Searching*, 112–35; Janssen, "Human Soul."
15. Wright, *Surprised by Hope*, 149–53.
16. Murphy and Green, *Whatever Happened*, 25–29.

- Hope in resurrection: The conditionalist view encourages hope in God's promise of resurrection for each soul-print, not inherent immortality (1 Cor 15:53–54).
- Ethical living: Recognizing the soul-print's value as God-given experience motivates ethical choices that honor divine will (Matt 16:26).

CONCLUSION

The conditionalist view of the soul, as the nonmaterial soul-print of human experience contingent on God's sustenance, offers a biblically grounded alternative to traditional dualism. Supported by Scripture and theological voices from Irenaeus to N. T. Wright, this perspective emphasizes the soul-print's dependence on divine life and its hope in resurrection. It calls believers to live in relationship with God, trusting his preservation and reconstitution of their unique identity in the resurrection.

10

A Biblical and Theological Critique of the Arbitrary Use of the Term "Remnant"

THE BIBLICAL DEFINITION AND THEOLOGICAL WEIGHT OF "REMNANT"

THE TERM "REMNANT" (HEBREW *she'ar, sha'rit* or Greek *hupoleimma, leimma*) in Scripture carries precise theological weight that resists modern appropriation. The Hebrew *she'ar* (שְׁאָר) appears 132 times in the Old Testament, consistently describing what survives divine judgment—whether Noah's family preserved through floodwaters (Gen 7:23) or the "very small remnant" of Judah after exile (Isa 1:9). This survival is never portrayed as human achievement but as divine intervention—the "tenth" that remains being holy seed (Isa 6:13).

The Septuagint translators carefully rendered these concepts with Greek terms carrying distinct connotations: *hupoleimma* (ὑπόλειμμα) in Isa 10:22 and Rom 9:27 implies something left behind after subtraction, while *leimma* (λεῖμμα) in Rom 11:5 suggests a deliberate remainder. These technical distinctions matter profoundly when examining:

- Isaiah 10:20–23's description of a remnant returning to God after judgment, emphasizing divine faithfulness to a repentant few.

- Romans 9:27–29's citation of Isaiah to underscore sovereign election, where remnant status derives from God's call, not human merit.
- Revelation 12:17's use of *loipoi* (λοιποί)—a generic term for "the rest"—rather than the covenantal *hupoleimma*. This linguistic shift indicates John describes faithful believers generally, not a theologically exclusive group.[1]

The arbitrary use of "remnant" to claim denominational exclusivity violates these textual boundaries. By conflating *loipoi* with *hupoleimma*, some groups misread Rev 12:17 as institutional prophecy rather than a description of persecuted faithfulness. This disregards Paul's admonition in 2 Tim 2:15 on "accurately handling the word of truth."

THE REMNANT THROUGH SALVATION HISTORY

The remnant motif pulses through Scripture's narrative as a rhythmic refrain of divine preservation. After Adam's fall, Seth's line maintains true worship (Gen 4:26). Post-Babel, Abraham receives the covenant promise (Gen 12:1–3). Elijah's despair at being "alone" is corrected by God's preservation of seven thousand (1 Kgs 19:18)—a pattern recurring through every covenantal crisis.

This historical trajectory exposes the fallacy of denominational exclusivity claims:

- In Rom 11:5, Paul's "remnant according to God's gracious choice" emphasizes divine election over human affiliation.
- The New Testament radicalizes the motif: Jesus declares the meek will "inherit the earth" (Matt 5:5), repurposing Ps 37's remnant language for the transnational kingdom.
- Paul's olive tree metaphor (Rom 11:17–24) stretches remnant theology to include wild gentile branches, while Revelation's persecuted saints (Rev 12:17) embody a faith-marked people, not institutionally-defined adherents.[2]

---

1. Beale, *Book of Revelation*, 668.
2. Bauckham, *Theology*, 68.

THEOLOGICAL MISUSE OF "REMNANT" AS A SECTARIAN LABEL

Theologically, the remnant motif in Scripture is about God's grace and preservation, not human achievement or denominational purity. For instance:

- In Rom 11:5, Paul speaks of a "remnant according to God's gracious choice," emphasizing divine election over self-selection. Claiming the remnant title arbitrarily shifts the focus from God's initiative to human ideology.[3]
- The New Testament broadens the remnant concept to include both Jews and gentiles in the church (Rom 11:17–24; Eph 2:11–22). Applying it exclusively to one denomination contradicts the universal scope of the gospel, which unites all believers in Christ (Gal 3:28; cf. Col 3:11, where distinctions are abolished in Christ).

Some denominations use the "remnant" label to distinguish themselves as the sole faithful group, often tying it to specific doctrines or practices (e.g., Sabbath-keeping or prophetic interpretations). This approach risks sectarianism, which Jesus warned against in John 17:20–21, where he prayed for the unity of all believers. Theologically, such exclusivity undermines the doctrine of the *ekklesia* as the universal body of Christ (1 Cor 12:12–27).[4]

Further, they overstep their bounds by creating a Christological hermeneutic where there is none. In the absence of a New Testament text that interprets the Old Testament as forecasting an eschatological remnant bearing "identifying marks"[5] that "keep the commandments of God and hold to the testimony of Jesus" (Rev 12:17), what remains is a religious construction informed by a priori assumptions undergirded by eisegesis. Further exacerbating the overreach is the idea that the expression "spirit of prophecy" refers to the writings of Ellen G. White (1827–1915). This co-opted designation has an interesting history.

---

3. Fee, *Paul*, 123.
4. Keener, *Revelation*, 322.
5. General Conference on Seventh-Day Adventists, *Seventh-day Adventists*, 153.

CRITIQUE OF THE "BOLT OF CLOTH" ANALOGY

Alluding to the Seventh-day Adventist (SDA) Church, Mark Finley, former host of *It Is Written*, states,

> In simple terms, a remnant is what is left over. If you purchase three yards of material from a fabric store for a dress or suit and you have a one-foot piece left over, that one-foot piece is the remnant. It is the last part of the original. In biblical terms, God's last-day church is the remnant. It is the last part of the original New Testament church. It keeps the faith of Jesus in the context of the last days of earth's history.[6]

The analogy of the remnant as the last part of material on a bolt of cloth, used to suggest a specific denomination in the last days, lacks biblical grounding and relies on a faulty exegesis of Rev 12:17. This interpretation imposes a modern, non-scriptural image onto the text, violating the principle of letting Scripture interpret itself (*sola scriptura*). As Peter warns in 2 Pet 1:20–21, "But know this first of all, that no prophecy of Scripture is a matter of one's own interpretation, for no prophecy was ever made by an act of human will, but men moved by the Holy Spirit spoke from God." The "bolt of cloth" imagery is a human construct, not derived from the text's historical or grammatical context, and it distorts the meaning of *loipoi* as a general reference to faithful believers.[7]

THE CO-OPTING OF "SPIRIT OF PROPHECY" FROM REVELATION 19:10: JUSTIFICATION AND CRITICISM BY SDA AND NON-SDA THEOLOGIANS

The arbitrary application of the "remnant" label by groups like the Seventh-day Adventist Church is closely tied to their use of the designation "Spirit of Prophecy," derived from Rev 19:10, which states, "For the testimony of Jesus is the spirit of prophecy." Ellen G. White and the SDA Church have co-opted this phrase to describe her writings as a modern manifestation of the prophetic gift, positioning them as authoritative guidance for the church while subordinate to Scripture. This usage is justified by SDA theologians as a biblical fulfillment for the end times

---

6. Finley, *Last Generation*, 49.
7. Beale, *Book of Revelation*, 669.

but criticized by both SDA and non-SDA scholars for potentially elevating extrabiblical authority, risking doctrinal dependency, and lacking scriptural warrant. The following analysis draws on perspectives from SDA and non-SDA theologians, highlighting justifications and criticisms.

Justification by SDA Theologians

SDA theologians justify the co-opting of "Spirit of Prophecy" by linking Rev 19:10 (and Rev 12:17) to the end-time remnant church, arguing that White's ministry fulfills the prophetic gift described in the New Testament (e.g., 1 Cor 12:28; Eph 4:11). George R. Knight, in *Ellen White's World*, contends that the term refers to ongoing prophetic guidance for God's people, with White's writings serving as a "lesser light" to illuminate Scripture, unifying the church around distinctive doctrines like the Sabbath and health reform without adding new revelation.[8] Herbert E. Douglass, in *Messenger of the Lord*, asserts that White meets biblical tests of prophecy (Deut 18:22; 1 John 4:1–3), and the designation from Rev 19:10 validates her role in providing inspired counsel for spiritual and practical living in the last days.[9] Alberto R. Timm, associated with the Ellen G. White Estate, emphasizes that the "Spirit of Prophecy" integrates biblical truths contextually, reinforcing the *ekklesia*'s identity as a faithful remnant and supporting institutional growth through mission and education.[10]

Criticism by SDA Theologians

While SDA theologians generally affirm the designation, some internal criticism exists, often from progressive or former members who question its application. Woodrow W. Whidden, in *Ellen White on Salvation*, critiques the overemphasis on White's writings as the "Spirit of Prophecy," arguing it can lead to legalism and doctrinal rigidity, potentially overshadowing grace-centered theology.[11] George Knight himself, in

---

8. Knight, *Ellen White's World*, 45–67.
9. Douglass, *Messenger of the Lord*, 112–35.
10. Timm, "Spirit of Prophecy," 1245–48.
11. Whidden, *Ellen White on Salvation*, 78–92.

Reading Ellen White, warns against treating her writings as infallible or using the "Spirit of Prophecy" label to enforce uniformity, noting that White encouraged contextual application rather than literalism.[12] Alden Thompson, in *Escape from the Flames*, argues that the co-opting risks elevating White to quasi-canonical status, which she opposed, and calls for a more nuanced view where her writings are inspirational but not the definitive interpretation of Scripture.[13]

Justification by Non-SDA Theologians

Non-SDA theologians rarely justify the co-opting, but some acknowledge its devotional value. Geoffrey J. Paxton, an Anglican theologian, in *The Shaking of Adventism*, defends the "Spirit of Prophecy" as a legitimate expression of charismatic guidance, arguing it aligns with Protestant views of ongoing revelation if subordinate to Scripture, and he notes it strengthens SDA identity without necessitating criticism.[14] Similarly, Anthony A. Hoekema, in a revised assessment, recognizes that if the designation is used for inspiration rather than authority, it parallels other denominational founders like John Wesley, justifying it as a tool for unity.[15]

Criticism by Non-SDA Theologians

Non-SDA theologians predominantly criticize the co-opting as an overinterpretation of Rev 19:10, risking cultlike dependency. Walter Martin, in *The Kingdom of the Cults*, argues that applying "Spirit of Prophecy" to White elevates her writings to near-scriptural status, undermining *sola scriptura* and aligning SDA with exclusivist sects.[16] Dale Ratzlaff, a former Seventh-day Adventist who is now evangelical, in *The Cultic Doctrine of Seventh-day Adventists*, condemns it as doctrinal manipulation, claiming White's failed prophecies (e.g., 1844 "shut door") fail

---

12. Knight, *Reading Ellen White*, 34–56.
13. Thompson, *Escape from the Flames*, 145–60.
14. Paxton, *Shaking of Adventism*, 89–104.
15. Hoekema, *Four Major Cults*, 120–35.
16. Martin, *Kingdom of the Cults*, 517–45.

biblical tests, making the designation unbiblical.[17] Hank Hanegraaff, in *Christianity in Crisis: 21st Century*, criticizes it as false prophecy, arguing Rev 19:10 refers to the testimony of Jesus, not a modern prophet, and warns it fosters legalism.[18] Anthony A. Hoekema, in *The Four Major Cults*, views it as subordinating Scripture to prophetic interpretation, conflicting with Protestant principles.[19]

This critique connects directly to the broader issue of arbitrary remnant claims, as the SDA's use of "Spirit of Prophecy" often undergirds their exclusive remnant identity, relying on eisegesis to link White's writings to Rev 12:17's "testimony of Jesus." Such interpretive practices further illustrate the dangers of imposing human constructs onto biblical texts, as seen in the "bolt of cloth" analogy.

CONTEXTUAL MISREADING OF REVELATION 12:17

Revelation 12:17 describes the dragon's war against "the rest of [the woman's] offspring," identified as those who keep God's commandments and hold to Jesus' testimony. The broader context of Rev 12 depicts a cosmic conflict between Satan and God's people, symbolized by the woman (often interpreted as Israel, the church, or God's covenant people). The "rest" (*loipoi*) likely refers to all faithful Christians enduring persecution, not a single denomination. Claiming this verse as a denominational marker ignores:

- The apocalyptic genre of Revelation, which uses symbolic language to convey universal truths, not specific denominational identities (Rev 1:1–3).

- The inclusive nature of the "testimony of Jesus," which applies to all believers (Rev 1:2, 9; Rev 19:10; cf. Rev 14:12, where faithful saints are similarly described).

- The absence of any denominational specificity in the text itself.

---

17. Ratzlaff, *Cultic Doctrine*, 210–35.
18. Hanegraaff, *Christianity in Crisis*, 312–28.
19. Hoekema, *Four Major Cults*, 120–35.

A BIBLICAL AND THEOLOGICAL CRITIQUE

DANGERS OF SECTARIAN EXEGESIS

The phrase "building a human out of a pig's tooth" vividly illustrates the error of constructing a theology from a misreading of a single term.[20] This practice reflects eisegesis (reading into the text) rather than exegesis (drawing meaning from the text). Such approaches:

- Foster division within the body of Christ, contrary to Eph 4:3–6, which calls for unity in "one body and one Spirit" (v. 4).

- Misrepresent God's redemptive plan, which is inclusive of all who trust in Christ, not limited to one group (John 3:16; Acts 10:34–35; cf. Rom 10:12–13, where salvation is for all who call on the Lord).

- Risk spiritual pride, as Jesus critiqued in the Pharisees' self-righteous exclusivity (Luke 18:9–14).[21]

BIBLICAL PRINCIPLES FOR CORRECT INTERPRETATION

To avoid arbitrary uses of "remnant," biblical interpretation should adhere to:

- Contextual analysis: Interpret terms like "remnant" or "rest" within their immediate literary and historical context (e.g., Isaiah's remnant as a post-exilic group, Revelation's *loipoi* as persecuted believers).[22]

- Canonical consistency: Ensure interpretations align with the broader biblical narrative, such as the universal call to salvation (Rom 10:12–13; cf. Acts 15:11, where salvation through grace unites Jews and gentiles).

- Humility: Recognize that no single group monopolizes God's truth, as all believers are part of Christ's body (1 Cor 12:27; cf. Eph 1:22–23, where Christ is head of the universal church).

---

20. Barth, *Church Dogmatics*, 2/1, 109.
21. Bauckham, *Theology*, 96.
22. Fee and Stuart, *How to Read*, 27.

CONCLUSION

The arbitrary use of "remnant" to claim denominational exclusivity misinterprets biblical texts like Rev 12:17, ignores linguistic distinctions (e.g., *loipoi* vs. *hupoleimma*), and imposes human assumptions onto Scripture. Theologically, it undermines the unity of the *ekklesia* and God's inclusive grace. Faithful exegesis requires humility, contextual accuracy, and alignment with the broader biblical narrative, ensuring that no group claims the remnant title as a pretext for sectarianism.

11

The *Ekklesia* vs. the Institutional Church
Visibility, Identity, and Divine Recognition

THE DISTINCTION BETWEEN THE *ekklesia*[1] and the institutional church is more than semantic—it is ontological, theological, and eschatological. This chapter explores the biblical and theological identity of the *ekklesia* as distinct from ecclesiastical structures, tracing the tension between its spiritual essence and institutional forms. Like a vine intertwined with a trellis, the *ekklesia* grows organically through divine life, while the institution provides structure that can either support or constrain its flourishing. Here, the true people of God are recognizable not by denominational affiliation or institutional hierarchy, but by their union with Christ, their participation in his body, and their discernible presence as "salt and light" in the world (Matt 5:13–16; John 17:20–23).

While the term "church" has become synonymous with buildings, denominations, and organizational frameworks, the New Testament usage of *ekklesia* refers primarily to the called-out community of believers who are in vital, covenantal relationship with the risen Christ. This chapter will argue that Jesus knows those who are his (2 Tim 2:19), that his sheep hear his voice (John 10:27), and that these relational and spiritual markers outweigh institutional boundaries. The *ekklesia*

---

1. The New Testament Greek term *ekklesia* is used here to emphasize the called-out community of believers in contrast to the institutional church.

is invisible only organizationally but profoundly visible in the world through faithful witness, obedience, and sanctified presence.

BIBLICAL FOUNDATIONS

The Greek feminine noun *ekklesia* appears over 100 times in the New Testament and never refers to a physical building or religious bureaucracy. It is derived from the Greek verb *ekkaleo*, meaning "to call out," and denotes those summoned by God for a specific purpose (cf. Acts 7:38; Matt 16:18). Jesus declared, "I will build My church [*ekklesia*]; and the gates of Hades will not overpower it" (Matt 16:18).[2] His statement is both declarative and prophetic. He does not speak of constructing an institution but of forming a people who live in dynamic relationship with him.

In John 10:14, Jesus states, "I am the good shepherd, and I know My own, and My own know Me." This intimate relational knowing is a defining characteristic of the *ekklesia*. In 2 Tim 2:19, Paul echoes this theme: "The Lord knows those who are His." These verses distinguish between outward affiliation and inward belonging. The true *ekklesia* is known by God's recognition and not human registration.

The *ekklesia* is described as the body (1 Cor 12:12–27), the building (Eph 2:20–22), and the bride of Christ (Rev 21:2; Eph 5:25–27). Each metaphor reveals a different dimension of ecclesial identity: relational unity, spiritual structure, and covenantal intimacy. The body metaphor stresses interdependence; the building metaphor emphasizes divine habitation; and the bride metaphor highlights exclusive covenant loyalty. Nowhere are these metaphors contingent upon denominational labels or institutional forms.

Furthermore, in John 17:21–23, Jesus prays that his followers "may all be one; just as You, Father, are in Me and I in You, that they also may be in Us, so that the world may believe that You sent Me." The oneness for which Christ prays is not administrative but ontological—a oneness grounded in shared life with the Father through the Son (Eph 4:1–6). Paul's exhortation to maintain "the unity of the Spirit in the bond of peace" (Eph 4:3) underscores that this oneness is a divine gift, not a

---

2. Although English translations use the pronoun "it" in this verse, the Greek text uses the uses the genitive feminine third-person singular pronoun, αὐτῆς.

human achievement. This unity serves as a visible witness in the world and underscores the *ekklesia*'s presence as salt and light (Matt 5:13–16).

In Rev 2–3, Jesus addresses "the churches" with intimate knowledge of their faithfulness and/or lack thereof. He calls them to overcome, indicating that true membership in the *ekklesia* is validated through spiritual perseverance, not institutional recognition. This reinforces the view that the *ekklesia* is visible not in title, but in faithfulness, rendering denominational labels and the attributions to them redundant.

ETYMOLOGICAL AND HISTORICAL DEVELOPMENT

Having established the scriptural foundations of the *ekklesia*'s identity, we now explore its etymological roots and historical development, tracing the tension between its spiritual essence and institutional forms.

The term "church" has a complex etymological history that illuminates its divergence from the New Testament's *ekklesia*. Likely derived from the Greek *kyriakon*, meaning "of the Lord" (from *kyrios*, "lord" or "master"), the phrase *kyriakon doma* referred to "the Lord's house."[3] This term was adopted by the Goths, who rendered it into Proto-Germanic as *kirika*, which evolved into Old English *cirice* or *circe*, out of which we get the word "circus," then Middle English *chirche*, and finally modern English "church." Cognates appear across Germanic languages, such as German *Kirche*, Dutch *kerk*, Scots *kirk*, and Old Norse *kirkja*, reflecting a shared linguistic heritage.[4]

In early Christian usage, *kyriakon* described places of worship, but the New Testament primarily used *ekklesia* (from *ekkaleo*, "to call out") to denote the assembly of believers summoned by God, as seen in Matt 16:18. Notably, *ekklesia* was also used for secular assemblies, such as the riotous gathering in Ephesus described as an *ekklesia* (Acts 19:32), indicating a local council or assembly, not necessarily religious in nature. This distinction is critical: *ekklesia* emphasized the community of the called-out ones, not a physical structure or institution.[5] After Christianity's institutionalization in the Roman Empire following the Constantinian shift in the fourth century, *kyriakon* gained prominence as a

---

3. Holweck, "Church (Etymology of the Word)," 744–45.
4. Kittel and Friedrich, *Theological Dictionary*, 2:501–36.
5. Kittel and Friedrich, *Theological Dictionary*, 2:501–36.

term for the buildings where Christians gathered, gradually obscuring the organic nature of *ekklesia*.[6] By the medieval period, "church" had expanded to encompass not only physical structures but also the hierarchical institution of Christianity, particularly in Western Europe.[7]

The Protestant Reformation sought—unsuccessfully—to reclaim the biblical *ekklesia*, emphasizing the spiritual body of believers over ecclesiastical structures. Reformers like Martin Luther and John Calvin critiqued the institutional excesses of the medieval church, focusing on the community formed by the word and Spirit.[8] The post-apostolic period reveals an early church that understood itself not as a political institution but as a pilgrim people. The *Didache* and the writings of Ignatius of Antioch emphasize holiness, love, and faithfulness rather than ecclesial power.[9] Clement of Rome described the church as a spiritual organism governed by Christ's rule and the witness of apostolic tradition.[10]

With the Constantinian shift in the fourth century, the church transitioned from persecuted minority to state-supported entity. This institutionalization created a structural hierarchy that began to obscure the organic nature of the *ekklesia*. Augustine's doctrine of the *corpus permixtum*—the mingling of true and false believers within the church—reflects his awareness that institutional membership alone could not signify true belonging to Christ.[11]

The medieval period further conflated ecclesiastical power with spiritual authority. Reformers like Martin Luther and John Calvin sought to reclaim the identity of the church as grounded in the word of God and the faithful preaching of the gospel. Luther's insistence on the "priesthood of all believers" and Calvin's emphasis on the marks of the true church (word, sacrament, and discipline) attempted to recover a biblical ecclesiology against institutional excesses.[12]

---

6. González, *Story of Christianity*, 91–104.

7. González, *Story of Christianity*, 256–78.

8. Luther, "Babylonian Captivity"; Calvin, *Institutes*, 4.1.1–4.2.12.

9. For the *Didache*, see 1.1—6.2. For Ignatius of Antioch, see *Letter to the Ephesians*, 2.2–3.2 and 4.1–5.2; *Letter to the Magnesians*, 6.1–7.2; *Letter to the Trallians*, 2.1–3.2. These texts consistently prioritize virtues like unity in love and holiness over hierarchical authority.

10. Clement of Rome, *1 Clement*.

11. Augustine, *City of God*, trans. Bettenson, 20.9 (915–17).

12. Luther, "Babylonian Captivity," 94; Calvin, *Institutes*, 4.1.9–10.

Anabaptists, often marginalized and persecuted, emphasized voluntary membership, believers' baptism, and communal accountability—hallmarks of the *ekklesia*. Their vision stood in contrast to both Catholic and Magisterial Protestant models. Similarly, Radical Pietists and later Holiness movements stressed spiritual rebirth over formal affiliation.

In the modern era, ecclesiology has continued to evolve, but fragmentation has often led to further conflation of the *ekklesia* with institutional brands. Nonetheless, theologians like Karl Barth, Lesslie Newbigin, and Stanley Hauerwas have continued to affirm the visible witness of the *ekklesia* as a counterculture community formed by the gospel and distinct from worldly systems.[13] Today, unlike *ekklesia*, which is delimited organically as the called-out people of God (Matt 16:18), "church" can refer to a building, a denomination (e.g., Catholic Church), the global Christian community, or a local congregation, often conflating these distinct realities.

SYSTEMATIC THEOLOGICAL ANALYSIS

From the standpoint of systematic theology, the nature of the *ekklesia* must be grounded in the doctrine of God, Christology, pneumatology, and eschatology. The *ekklesia* exists because God is a covenant-making and covenant-keeping God. As the redeemed people of God, the *ekklesia* reflects the triune nature of God—called by the Father, redeemed by the Son, and sanctified by the Spirit of God (Eph 1:3–14).

Christologically, the *ekklesia* is the mystical body of Christ (1 Cor 12:27; Eph 5:23). Its unity is forged by the shared life of Christ through the Spirit. In Eph 1:22–23, Paul describes the *ekklesia* as "the fullness of Him who fills all in all." This mystical union surpasses institutional affiliation and depends entirely on one's participation in Christ's redemptive work (Rom 6:5; Col 1:18).

Pneumatologically, the Holy Spirit constitutes and empowers the *ekklesia*. In Acts 2, the descent of the Spirit inaugurates a Spirit-formed community bearing witness to Christ in word and deed. The fruit of the Spirit (Gal 5:22–23) and the manifestations of the Spirit (1 Cor 12)

---

13. Barth, *Church Dogmatics*, 4/3.1, 650–725; Newbigin, *Gospel in a Pluralist*, 222–33; Hauerwas, *Community of Character*, 84–99.

are evidences of authentic participation in the *ekklesia*. These are not contingent on ordination or hierarchy but on spiritual regeneration.

Eschatologically, the *ekklesia* is the bride of Christ being prepared for glorification (Rev 19:7–9). The "church militant," meaning the *ekklesia* at war, is not coextensive with the institutional church. The elect is known by God and will be gathered by Christ at his return (Matt 24:31). This reinforces the reality that the *ekklesia* exists within and sometimes despite the institutions, and its legitimacy is determined by divine recognition, not clerical endorsement.

Theologically, then, the *ekklesia* cannot be reduced to a sociological phenomenon or bureaucratic mechanism. It is a transcendent, Spirit-formed reality that breaks into history and bears witness to the kingdom of God. It remains visible and active (1 Cor 15:58).

CONTEMPORARY IMPLICATIONS

In today's ecclesial landscape, the distinction between the *ekklesia* and the institutional church is not only theological but deeply practical. Many believers experience disillusionment with denominational structures, including their prioritization of survival over sanctification, politics over prophecy, and branding over biblical fidelity. The *ekklesia* remains the locus of divine action, even as the institutions falter.

Movements such as the house church revival, underground churches in restricted countries, and decentralized fellowships echo the early *ekklesia* in spirit and form. They demonstrate that spiritual vitality does not require formal infrastructure. What matters most is faithfulness to Christ, obedience to Scripture, and openness to the Spirit's leading (John 4:23–24).

The moral crises within some churches—scandals, cover-ups, and politicized pulpits—reveal a widening chasm between institutional allegiance and spiritual authenticity. The *ekklesia* persists because Christ sustains her (Matt 28:20). She thrives in obscurity, among the persecuted, the marginalized, and the faithful remnant (Heb 11:36–38).

Kelly Brown Douglas, in *Stand Your Ground*, exposes the institutional church's complicity in systemic injustice, particularly its alignment with racial oppression, which betrays the *ekklesia*'s calling to be salt and light in a world marred by inequity.[14] Douglas argues that the

---

14. Douglas, *Stand Your Ground*.

church's failure to confront the "stand-your-ground" culture of violence and exclusion undermines its prophetic witness, leaving the *ekklesia* to embody justice and love among those the institution often overlooks. Her critique illuminates the necessity of discerning the *ekklesia* as a community unbound by institutional compromise, standing in solidarity with the oppressed as a beacon of God's kingdom.

Similarly, James Cone, in *The Cross and the Lynching Tree*, draws a searing parallel between Christ's crucifixion and the lynching of Black bodies, revealing the *ekklesia*'s identity as a community of resistance forged in the crucible of suffering.[15] Cone critiques the institutional Church's silence during centuries of racial violence, noting that true ecclesial witness emerges among the marginalized, where the Spirit moves in defiance of worldly powers. The *ekklesia*, as Cone envisions, is not found in the grandeur of cathedrals but in the resilient faith of those who, like Christ, bear the cross of injustice, embodying the hope of resurrection.

The White evangelical church has aligned itself with Christian nationalism and by so doing perpetuates its betrayal of the Christian ethic. Its historical roots of complicity in slavery, racism, and segregation have yet to be atoned for and it continues to diminish its credibility as a human institution. It bears little resemblance, if any, to the *ekklesia*.

For modern disciples, the call is not necessarily to abandon the institutional church, but at a minimum to discern the *ekklesia* within and beyond it. This requires spiritual clarity and theological courage. As Bonhoeffer warned, "The Church is the Church only when it exists for others."[16] Institutional inertia must give way to Spirit-formed mission.

Finally, recognizing the *ekklesia* is critical in a pluralistic age. The "church" is defined by attributions, social consensus, and doctrinal minimalism rather than by its covenantal union with Christ. Even in the misrepresentation of the *ekklesia* as the "church," common English parlance prefers "it" over "her," the neuter over the feminine, contributing to the dissipation of the covenant relationship. The purpose of the covenant is to bear public witness to how believers live, love, and endure. The world does not need more identity confusion or denominational logos—it needs to see the body of Christ in motion (Phil 2:15–16).

---

15. Cone, *Cross*.
16. Bonhoeffer, *Letters and Papers*, 382.

ADDITIONAL DISTINCTIONS: BODY, BUILDING, AND BRIDE

The New Testament describes the *ekklesia* with a triad of metaphors that convey its theological richness and functional purpose: the body of Christ, the building of God, and the bride of Christ. Each of these designations carries specific implications about identity, relationality, and divine initiative.

As the body of Christ (1 Cor 12:12–27; Rom 12:4–5), the *ekklesia* is a living organism comprised of diverse members unified by one Spirit. Paul's language emphasizes interdependence and mutual edification. No member exists in isolation, and the health of the body depends on the functional faithfulness of each part (Eph 4:11–16). This vision rebukes hierarchical models and their top-heavy concentration of authority, and instead prioritizes the work of the Spirit and shared vocation.

As the building of God (Eph 2:19–22; 1 Pet 2:4–5), the *ekklesia* is depicted as a spiritual temple, constructed upon the foundation of the apostles and prophets, with Christ as the cornerstone. The community is being "built together into a dwelling of God in the Spirit" (Eph 2:22). This underscores divine agency—God does the building—and also implies progressive formation. The *ekklesia* is under construction, and its architecture is holy.

As the bride of Christ (Eph 5:25–27; Rev 19:7–9; 21:2), the *ekklesia* is defined by covenantal intimacy. Christ loves the *ekklesia* and gave himself for her, not as a mere institution, but as a relational partner. The imagery of marriage conveys exclusivity, faithfulness, and future consummation. This eschatological union guides the *ekklesia*'s present purity and longing. The bride metaphor also distinguishes the *ekklesia* from all other affiliations—she belongs to no one but Christ.

These metaphors are never used interchangeably with any denomination or clerical structure in Scripture. Instead, they describe a transcendent reality that is visible in faithfulness, love, and obedience to Christ. The body functions, the building houses divine presence, and the bride prepares herself for union. This triple identity reminds the *ekklesia* of her divine origin, purpose, and destiny.

THEOLOGICAL CHALLENGES AND POLEMICS

The distinction between the *ekklesia* and the institutional church is not without controversy. Many scholars and ecclesial leaders view the critique of institutionalism as subversive or divisive. However, Scripture consistently distinguishes between nominal and authentic faith communities (Matt 7:21-23; Rev 3:1). The prophetic tradition, from Isaiah to Jesus, rebukes formal religion devoid of covenantal fidelity (Isa 1:11-17; Matt 23).

One theological challenge arises from conflating visibility with legitimacy. Some argue that the visible institutional church must be equated with the body of Christ, citing early patristic statements such as Cyprian's *extra ecclesiam nulla salus* ("outside the church there is no salvation").[17] Yet even Cyprian recognized the spiritual nature of true communion, and Augustine's concept of the *corpus permixtum* (mixed body) acknowledged that wheat and tares coexist in the church until the eschaton (Matt 13:24-30).[18]

Modern ecclesiologies sometimes err by reducing the church to either sociological form or private spirituality. Liberal Protestantism has tended to align the church with cultural accommodation, while hyper-individualistic evangelicalism risks detaching believers from communal accountability. Both extremes undermine the robust biblical identity of the *ekklesia* as a visible, holy, covenantal people.

The challenge of defining the *ekklesia* in pluralistic contexts is compounded by ecclesial consumerism, celebrity pastoralism, and the politicization of faith. The New Testament warns against false teachers, hirelings, and wolves in sheep's clothing (John 10:12; 2 Pet 2:1-3). A return to the biblical model requires theological discernment, spiritual maturity, and a willingness to separate fidelity to Christ from allegiance to human systems.

Ultimately, the polemic is against the idea of church governance, structure, and community as if it is the *ekklesia*; it is against the idolatry of the institution as an end in itself. The church is not to be confused with the *ekklesia* if for no other reason, the notion of the church assumes a unified body, but there is no basis for such an assumption with approximately forty-one thousand to forty-five thousand Protestant bodies

---

17. Cyprian, *On the Unity*, 423.
18. Augustine, *City of God*, trans. Dyson, 20.9 (1016).

alone worldwide. The *ekklesia* has one Lord, one faith, and one baptism; and its head is Christ (Eph 4:5; Eph 1:21–23; Col 1:18; Eph 5:23).

ORGANIZATIONAL ASSUMPTION: THE JERUSALEM COUNCIL

While many scholars affirm the Jerusalem Council (Acts 15:1–35; cf. Gal 2:1–10) as a foundational moment for early church structure, they may overlook how Paul's descriptions of the *ekklesia* as the body of Christ (Col 1:13–18; 1 Cor 12:12–14; Rom 12:4–5) challenge the traditional hierarchical ecclesiology potentially seeded by the council's authority. In fact, while not dismissing organic unity, the apostle Paul advocates—through the use of metaphor—a nonhierarchical, Spirit-led organization over which Christ is the head, countering centralized ecclesiastical control.[19]

Paul's exhortation in 1 Cor 12:31 to "desire the greater graces"[20]—referring to the Spirit's manifestations for the *ekklesia*'s benefit (1 Cor 12:7)—underscores a nonhierarchical model where all members contribute equally under Christ's headship (Col 1:18). This emphasis on Spirit-led diversity and mutual service may reflect Paul's response to hierarchical tendencies, such as those implied by the Jerusalem Council's authority, as explored in subsequent scholarly analyses.

Several Pauline scholars have examined Paul's interactions with the Jerusalem Council, as depicted in Acts 15 and Gal 2, highlighting tensions that suggest a reluctant compliance on his part. Robert Jewett portrays these interactions as complex negotiations over gentile inclusion, situating Paul's apostolic authority as independent of Jerusalem's oversight in his mission to house churches. F. F. Bruce describes Paul as cooperative, viewing the council as a strategic compromise for unity, though he acknowledges underlying strains evident in Paul's defensive assertions of independence in Galatians.[21] Anders Nygren, focusing on the Romans' theological framework, implicitly critiques any law-observant authority

---

19. Jewett, *Romans*, 59–72.
20. This is my translation of the Greek.
21. Bruce, *Paul*, 149–62.

from Jerusalem by emphasizing liberation through faith, aligning Paul's gospel with freedom from external impositions.[22]

N. T. Wright, in a chapter titled "New Perspective on Paul," interprets the council as affirming Paul's law-free gospel, while noting his defensive posture in Galatians as indicative of friction with the "pillars" of Jerusalem, suggesting a reluctant engagement to maintain broader unity.[23] James D. G. Dunn emphasizes significant ruptures, including Jerusalem's possible indifference to Paul's collection efforts and lack of support during his trials, portraying the council as exposing deep divisions where Paul resisted law-observant pressures to safeguard his mission.[24] Douglas Campbell views Paul as transcending ethnic-legal distinctions, treating Jerusalem's practices as negotiable in light of Christ's deliverance, with the council representing a controversial negotiation that Paul approached with underlying reluctance.[25]

Contributions from other notable scholars further illuminate this possibility. Ian J. Elmer argues that Paul's ecclesiology in these passages counters Jerusalem's separatist and law-observant tendencies, using the body metaphor to foster inclusive unity and resist divisions like those at Antioch, where Paul's confrontation with Peter under James's influence reflects strategic yet defensive submission.[26] Gordon D. Fee interprets 1 Cor 12 as subverting elitism, extending to anti-hierarchical themes that may include resistance to Jerusalem's apostolic claims, with Spirit-empowered gifts promoting equality over control.[27] The general scholarly consensus on the body metaphor notes Paul's subversion of ancient Greco-Roman hierarchical usages to advocate equality and mutual service, implicitly critiquing Jerusalem's "pillar" structure in Gal 2:9.[28]

In summary, Paul's depiction of the *ekklesia* as the body of Christ (Rom 12; 1 Cor 12; Col 1:13–18), emphasizing organic unity and Spirit-led diversity, aligns with scholarly views from Dunn, Wright, and Campbell on Paul's tensions with and reluctant navigation of Jerusalem's

22. Nygren, *Commentary on Romans*, 419–31.
23. Wright, *Paul and the Faithfulness*, 346–70.
24. Dunn, *Unity and Diversity*, 256–262.
25. Campbell, *Deliverance of God*, 156–85.
26. Elmer, *Paul, Jerusalem*, 123–45.
27. Fee, *First Epistle*, 650–78.
28. Elmer, *Paul, Jerusalem*, 123–45; Fee, *First Epistle*, 650–78; Jones, "Many Parts Yet One"; Braun, "Towards A Contextual Theology."

authority, challenging the hierarchical seeds of Acts 15. While some scholars, such as Bruce, view Paul's cooperation with the council as primarily strategic for unity, the tensions highlighted by Dunn, Wright, and others, combined with Paul's body metaphor, suggest a deliberate emphasis on a nonhierarchical *ekklesia* to counter centralized authority. By portraying the *ekklesia* as a body with Christ as head (Col 1:18), Paul promotes a decentralized model where Spirit-given graces (1 Cor 12:31) ensure mutual service, aligning with scholarly insights into his resistance against Jerusalem's centralized authority. These views are substantiated through exegesis of Paul's letters, emphasizing his revelatory independence (Gal 1:11–17) and ethical calls to mutual service.

CONCLUSION

The distinction between the *ekklesia* and the institutional church underscores that true authority resides with Christ as the head of his body, not within hierarchical structures or human institutions. Paul's depiction of the *ekklesia* as the body of Christ, emphasizing Spirit-led diversity and mutual service under Christ's headship (Col 1:18; 1 Cor 12:12–31; Rom 12:4–5), challenges the hierarchical assumptions potentially seeded by the Jerusalem Council (Acts 15:1–35). This perspective does not negate the role of denominations and ecclesiastical structures, which, like various vehicle brands, serve as imperfect instruments to facilitate the journey toward divine purposes. Analogously, institutional churches attract adherents based on liturgical practices, doctrinal emphases, or cultural alignment, yet their value lies not in inherent superiority but in their capacity to convey believers toward covenantal union with Christ.

This analogy highlights the transformative power of the cross, where Christ's assurance, "And I, if I am lifted up from the earth, will draw all men to Myself" (John 12:32), transcends institutional flaws. The biblical narrative demonstrates God's use of imperfect means—such as the humble donkey carrying Jesus into Jerusalem (Matt 21:1–11)—to achieve his redemptive ends. Similarly, institutional churches, despite their imperfections, encompass many within the *ekklesia* and extend the invitation to "other sheep" not yet within her fold (John 10:16). However, as scholars like Dunn, Wright, and Campbell suggest, Paul's emphasis on a nonhierarchical *Ekklesia* resists centralized authority, aligning with the witness of theologians like Douglas and Cone, who locate the *ekklesia*'s true identity among the marginalized and faithful, not in institutional grandeur. Thus, the *ekklesia* endures as the divinely recognized community, transcending institutional confines while manifesting through faithful witness, covenantal communion, and the Spirit's transformative power.

12

The Divine Image, Complementarity, and Women in Ministry

THE INSTITUTIONAL CHURCH AND THE ORDINATION DEBATE

THE QUESTION AS TO whether women can or should serve in ministry as official clergy assumes a whole lot relative to how the church is perceived. From the perspective of an institutional enterprise with a hierarchical structure, bound by a creed with membership, the prerequisites of which require fealty, the obvious answer is, "It depends!" If the traditions or cultural practices are superordinate then the answer will reflect it one way or another.

The vast majority of denominations that are still infighting about whether or not to ordain women are doing exactly what we should expect churches to do. There ought to be nothing strange about how social influence determines the outcome of matters within institutions that are intoxicated by attribution and that survive on the fuel of consensus.

The attribution grows out of a religiously constructed self-identity that borrows largely—in most cases—from the Bible and appropriates characteristics of the *ekklesia* along with a variety of prooftexts that

THE DIVINE IMAGE, COMPLEMENTARITY, AND WOMEN IN MINISTRY

explain why it has authority over the lives of its members. (I address the distinction between the church and the *ekklesia* later on in this chapter.) The consensus is simply the agreement of those who are employed by and/or hold membership in and defer to these institutions. In addition to attribution and consensus, the more historical the institution, generally the more legitimate it appears to be.

So, the fight over women's ordination in these contexts is legitimate if for no other reason than the premise. Catholic theologian Hans Küng appears, at least in part, to understand the premise. Küng's view of the church critiqued the emphasis on its visible aspects at the expense of spiritual aspects. He cited its structures, hierarchy, and regulations as being superordinate to the neglect of its spiritual ethos. He didn't reject the visible but highlighted the overemphasis on its outward forms to the neglect of the community—what he referred to as the "invisible Church."[1] In Küng's view, the Church is one, not two, but an imbalanced one struggling with its true nature.[2]

What Küng may not have realized is that the distinction between the organization (institutional church) and the organism (the body of Christ) is clear, at least from a biblical perspective. No doubt, he was influenced by tradition, which would ostensibly have made it difficult for him to see beyond the attributions of history and the consensus of his day. Unlike Küng's unified model, this distinction between organization and organism is clear to me and clearly the defining premise vis-à-vis women's ordination. The closest we come is in the use of five Greek words that similarly—howbeit in different contexts—mean "appoint."

- ποιέω (*poieo*): "to make" or "appoint," as in Mark 3:14, where Jesus "appointed" the twelve apostles.
- τάσσω (*tasso*): "to place in a certain order" or "appoint," as in Acts 13:48, where some translations render it as "ordained" to eternal life.
- χειροτονέω (*cheirotoneo*): "to appoint" or "to choose by raising of hands," used in Acts 14:23, where Paul and Barnabas "appointed" elders in the churches.
- καθίστημι (*kathistemi*): "to set in a certain order," "appoint," or "put in charge," used in Titus 1:5 regarding the appointment of elders.

1. Küng, *Church*, 3–22.
2. Küng, *Church*, 45.

- τίθημι (*tithemi*): "to put," "make," or "appoint," used in 1 Tim 2:7, where Paul describes being "appointed" as a preacher, apostle, and teacher.

There's no evidence that Jerome's translation of the Greek (Textus Receptus) in the Latin Vulgate remotely inferred any notion of "ordain" or the process of ordination. Notice:

- Greek (Textus Receptus): καὶ ἐποίησεν δώδεκα ("And he made twelve").
- Latin Vulgate: *Et fecit ut essent duodecim cum illo* ("And he made that twelve should be with him").

Wycliffe followed suit in his fourteenth-century translation (completed by 1395), but apparently the 1525 Tyndale Bible first translated the word "appoint" to read "ordain."[3] It stands to reason, as Tyndale was an ordained Catholic priest (London, 1515).[4] So, thanks to Tyndale, who sowed the seed of the tradition, ordination has, as a consequence of translation—as it was retained by the King James Version (KJV)—worked its way into the Bible and become established as a requirement for clerical ministry. In other words, the premise has become a pretext for discriminating against women, in the name of the church.

PROMINENT ROLES OF WOMEN IN SCRIPTURE AND THE *EKKLESIA*

The primacy of women in the funding of Jesus' ministry (Luke 8:1–3) and in being first to herald the risen Christ (Luke 24:1–12) has been widely written about, but consider that the prototypical disciple was the woman who anointed Jesus' feet with her hair and received as commendation: "She anointed My feet with perfume" (John 12:3) and "For when she poured this perfume on My body, she did it to prepare Me

---

3. The translation shift is most clearly seen in Titus 1:5. The Wycliffe Bible (c. 1395), translated from the Latin Vulgate, reads "ordeyne preestis," while William Tyndale's 1526 New Testament, translated from the Greek, first introduced the term "ordayne elders." For Wycliffe, see Forshall and Madden, *Holy Bible*, 4:623; for Tyndale, see Tyndale, *New Testament: A Facsimile*, fol. CCCXIIv.

4. Daniell, *William Tyndale*, 79.

for burial" (Matt 26:12). No male disciple received this honor or this commendation.

The significance of Mark 16:1–16 cannot be overlooked with respect to establishing what Peter would later emphasize on the day of Pentecost. Mark pulls no punches:

> When the Sabbath was over, Mary Magdalene, Mary the mother of James, and Salome bought spices so that they might come and anoint Him. And very early on the first day of the week, they came to the tomb when the sun had risen. They were saying to one another, "Who will roll away the stone from the entrance of the tomb for us?" And looking up, they noticed that the stone had been rolled away; for it was extremely large. And entering the tomb, they saw a young man sitting at the right, wearing a white robe; and they were amazed. But he said to them, "Do not be amazed; you are looking for Jesus the Nazarene, who has been crucified. He has risen; He is not here; see, here is the place where they laid Him. But go, tell His disciples and Peter, 'He is going ahead of you to Galilee; there you will see Him, just as He told you.'" And they went out and fled from the tomb, for trembling and astonishment had gripped them; and they said nothing to anyone, for they were afraid.
>
> Now after He had risen early on the first day of the week, He first appeared to Mary Magdalene, from whom He had cast out seven demons. She went and reported to those who had been with Him, while they were mourning and weeping. And when they heard that He was alive and had been seen by her, they refused to believe it.
>
> Now after that, He appeared in a different form to two of them while they were walking along on their way to the country. And they went away and reported it to the rest, but they did not believe them, either.
>
> Later He appeared to the eleven disciples themselves as they were reclining at the table; and He reprimanded them for their unbelief and hardness of heart, because they had not believed those who had seen Him after He had risen from the dead. And He said to them, "Go into all the world and preach the gospel to all creation. The one who has believed and has been baptized will be saved; but the one who has not believed will be condemned."
> (Mark 16:1–16)

To be clear, Mark 16:7, using the present active imperative (ὑπάγετε), establishes the commissioning of the women to proclaim the risen Christ. Verses 10, 11, and 14 underscore the fact of Jesus' commission of Mary Magdalene and the two disciples' faithfulness to their commission. In describing the responses of the disciples, Mark emphasizes unbelief (ἀπιστίαν) and hardness of heart (σκληροκαρδίαν), two words used descriptively of the disposition of the Jewish leaders but only ever co-joined here in Mark 16:14, giving some indication of the force of Jesus' rebuke.

On the day of Pentecost the prophecy of Joel 2:28–29 was fulfilled, guaranteeing that,

> It will come about after this
> That I will pour out My Spirit on all mankind;
> And your sons and your daughters will prophesy,
> Your old men will have dreams,
> Your young men will see visions.
> And even on the male and female servants
> I will pour out My Spirit in those days. (Joel 2:28–29)

What is determined in the church by tradition and/or custom is resolved in the *ekklesia*, where the only qualification for service of any kind is accepting Jesus as Lord and Savior. There are no hoops to jump through, no hierarchical steps to climb, and no creeds to swear an oath to, because an organism does not require those things; the unity is organic.

THE FALL, COMPLEMENTARITY, AND THE BY-PRODUCT OF EQUALITY

So, how did the picture get so twisted to begin with? It all goes back to the creation of Ha Adam (Adam and Eve) and God's intention concerning the nature of their relationship. In the absence of sin, God created Ha Adam (הָאָדָם) complementary, meaning as one. The pre-fall descriptions attest to the complementary relationship into which they were created. Notice how the writer of Genesis makes the contrast between humans and animals and how he uses the narrative to emphasize the complementary relationship:

> Then the Lord God said, "It is not good for the man to be alone; I will make him a helper suitable for him." And out of the ground the Lord God formed every animal of the field and every bird of the sky, and brought them to the man to see what he would call them; and whatever the man called a living creature, that was its

name. The man gave names to all the livestock, and to the birds of the sky, and to every animal of the field, but for Adam there was not found a helper suitable for him. So the Lord God caused a deep sleep to fall upon the man, and he slept; then He took one of his ribs and closed up the flesh at that place. And the Lord God fashioned into a woman the rib which He had taken from the man, and brought her to the man. The man said,
"This is now bone of my bones,
And flesh of my flesh;
She shall be called Woman,
Because she was taken out of Man."
For this reason a man shall leave his father and his mother, and be joined to his wife; and they shall become one flesh. And the man and his wife were both naked, but they were not ashamed. (Gen 2:18–25)

The key is verse 20, the last clause: "but for Adam there was not found a helper suitable for him." *Merriam-Webster* defines complementary as, "serving to fill out or complete," and "mutually supplying each other's lack."[5] This definition comes close to the pre-fall biblical ideal that Ha Adam was compatible in every way, and raises the question as to how the modern-day ideal has become equality.

The short answer is that one of the consequences of sin was the distortion of the complementary relationship, captured well in the omniscience of God, when he declared,

"I will greatly multiply
Your pain in childbirth,
In pain you shall deliver children;
Yet your desire will be for your husband,
And he shall rule over you." (Gen 3:16).

Consider the Hebrew terms: *teshuqah* (desire) appears only three times in the Hebrew Bible (Gen 3:16; 4:7; Song 7:10), often interpreted as a longing or turning toward. In Gen 3:16, it may signify the woman's yearning to restore pre-fall complementarity, disrupted by sin, rather than a desire to control (as some suggest). *Mashal* (rule) implies dominion, but in context, it describes the husband's post-fall inclination to dominate, not a prescriptive hierarchy. This intertextual reading with

---

5. *Merriam-Webster*, s.v. "complementary."

Gen 4:7 (where sin "desires" Cain but he must "rule" it) supports viewing Gen 3:16 as descriptive of relational tension, not eternal subordination.

The traditional interpretation of this verse (16b), sees it as describing the subordination of the woman to the man. It essentially treats 16b as an independent clause unconnected to 16a. Notice how the translation reads from popular versions:

> "I will surely multiply your pain in childbearing;
> in pain you shall bring forth children.
> Your desire shall be contrary to your husband,
> and he shall rule over you." (ESV)

> "I will make your pains in childbearing very severe;
> with painful labor you will give birth to children.
> Your desire will be for your husband,
> and he will rule over you." (NIV)

> "I will greatly increase your pain in childbirth. You will bring forth children in pain. Your desire will be toward your husband, but he will rule over you." (CJB)

> "I will intensify your labor pains;
> you will bear children with painful effort.
> Your desire will be for your husband,
> yet he will rule over you." (CSB)

Clearly, there is significant variance between the more popular translations, as they interpret the conjunction differently: *and, but, yet,* "he will rule over you." Each conjunction brings a different assumption to the interpretation and consequently results in a different meaning. Perhaps the one contextual framework in which any of the aforementioned conjunctions work is the complementary framework; it influences the interpretation of the text to mean, I will greatly multiply your pain in childbirth. In pain you shall deliver children; and, but, yet "your desire will be for your husband" (the desire to return to the complementary relationship), and "he shall rule over you"; the versions agree on the last clause.

Verse 16 begins when God announces that the woman's delivery pain will be greater, indicating that even before the fall, delivery involved some measure of pain. It continues presumably with a coordinating conjunction, "and," indicating continuity of thought rather than a contrasting thought as indicated by *but* or *yet*; "your desire will be for your husband." The woman's desire to return to the complementary relationship prior to the fall would be met by her husband's inclination to dominate her. That would constitute the post-fall natural order and would be manifested through patriarchy. It would evolve to become oppressive and exploitative and eventually elicit a backlash demonstrated by resistance, which evolved into, and continues as, the push for women's rights.[6]

This novel view contrasts with complementarian interpretations. For instance, John Piper argues that the woman's "desire" in Gen 3:16 is contrary to her husband, implying a desire to control him, countered by his God-ordained rule, introducing conflict into pre-fall roles.[7] Similarly, Wayne Grudem sees the verse as distorting roles, with male headship as a corrective to sin's effects, prohibiting women from authoritative ministry, as it reflects a created order of qualified male eldership.[8] These perspectives, while emphasizing biblical distinctions, overlook the pre-fall complementarity as oneness, treating hierarchy as normative rather than a distortion.

The quest for women's rights that focuses on equality is a response to social domination, where women have been devalued, used, and underpaid. They have historically been treated as a subspecies of man, less intelligent and less capable. Their common virtues have been caricatured and portrayed as weaknesses and liabilities, informing their unsuitability for ordination.

Complementarity would have voided any consideration of equality. Absent the fall, there would be no debate about equality. The current debate about equality vis-à-vis women's ordination takes place within the institution of the church, where there doesn't appear to be any consideration of the Gen 2 ideal. Genesis 3:16 has then become the church's pretext for the pretext of ordination. In fact, the quest for equality in the church institution is rightly placed and wholly appropriate. It is a fitting reminder of the measure in which human formulations can obfuscate the clear intent of Scripture.

---

6. Trible, *God and the Rhetoric*, 128–29.
7. Piper, *What's the Difference*, 36–38.
8. Grudem, *Evangelical Feminism*, 32–35.

ONENESS IN THE *EKKLESIA* AND MANIFESTATIONS OF THE SPIRIT

If on the other hand, women are content to recognize the limitations of the church as an institution/organization distinct from the organism (*ekklesia*), they will prefer to define their role and function in the body of Christ on the basis of 1 Cor 12:12–31:

> For just as the body is one and yet has many parts, and all the parts of the body, though they are many, are one body, so also is Christ. For by one Spirit we were all baptized into one body, whether Jews or Greeks, whether slaves or free, and we were all made to drink of one Spirit.
>
> For the body is not one part, but many. If the foot says, "Because I am not a hand, I am not a part of the body," it is not for this reason any less a part of the body. And if the ear says, "Because I am not an eye, I am not a part of the body," it is not for this reason any less a part of the body. If the whole body were an eye, where would the hearing be? If the whole body were hearing, where would the sense of smell be? But now God has arranged the parts, each one of them in the body, just as He desired. If they were all one part, where would the body be? But now there are many parts, but one body. And the eye cannot say to the hand, "I have no need of you"; or again, the head to the feet, "I have no need of you." On the contrary, it is much truer that the parts of the body which seem to be weaker are necessary; and those parts of the body which we consider less honorable, on these we bestow greater honor, and our less presentable parts become much more presentable, whereas our more presentable parts have no need of it. But God has so composed the body, giving more abundant honor to that part which lacked, so that there may be no division in the body, but that the parts may have the same care for one another. And if one part of the body suffers, all the parts suffer with it; if a part is honored, all the parts rejoice with it.
>
> Now you are Christ's body, and individually parts of it. And God has appointed in the church, first apostles, second prophets, third teachers, then miracles, then gifts of healings, helps, administrations, and various kinds of tongues. All are not apostles, are they? All are not prophets, are they? All are not teachers, are they? All are not workers of miracles, are they? All do not have gifts of healings, do they? All do not speak with tongues, do they? All do not interpret, do they? But earnestly desire the greater gifts. (1 Cor 12:12–31)

In 1 Cor 12:1, 7, 12–31, the exhortation is not about equality; it is about oneness in the *ekklesia*, where diverse manifestations of the Spirit unite believers under Christ's headship. The same can be said of Gal 3:28:

> There is neither Jew nor Greek, there is neither slave nor free, there is neither male nor female; for you are all one in Christ Jesus.

It is not about equality at all; it is about oneness. Equality is not only foreign to Paul's intent; it misses the mark by imposing a contemporary frame uncritically on the text. The oneness to which Paul appeals transcends post-fall distinctions, rendering debates over equality irrelevant in the *ekklesia*. Oneness presupposes that all of the parts of the body fulfilling different roles are necessary for functioning; the same can scarcely be said for equality.

Critics may argue that prioritizing oneness over equality diminishes biblical gender distinctions, particularly in passages like Eph 5:21–33, which allegedly describes mutual submission in marriage with the husband as head. While this issue is not the focus of this chapter, it is worth noting that verses 1–21 appear to emphasize mutual submission among the believers, as verse 1 strongly implies, and verses 22–33 focus on oneness, as verses 31 and 32 emphasize. However, this headship is not hierarchical dominance but a Christlike self-emptying self-giving that fosters oneness, mirroring the pre-fall complementarity. In the *ekklesia*, such distinctions serve unity rather than division; oneness does not erase roles but transcends post-fall distortions, ensuring all parts function interdependently under Christ (Eph 5:21: "Submit to one another out of reverence for Christ"). This defends against accusations of homogenization by emphasizing that oneness integrates diverse gifts without equality debates, as equality implies competition absent in organic unity.

MEMBERSHIP OVERLAP, PERMANENCE, AND TEMPORALITY

While the institutional church and the *ekklesia* are distinct in origin and nature, their memberships may intersect—believers in the *ekklesia* can participate in institutions, and institutional members may belong to the *ekklesia*. The *ekklesia*'s permanence (Matt 16:18), however, contrasts with the church's temporality, ensuring that true ministry endures beyond human structures.

> "That which has been born of the flesh is flesh, and that which has been born of the Spirit is spirit." (John 3:6)

The institutional church, as a flesh-born entity, is temporary and will eventually be overpowered, whereas the *ekklesia*, Spirit-born, remains unassailable.

ADDRESSING COUNTER-TEXTS IN THE CHURCH-*EKKLESIA* FRAMEWORK

Texts such as 1 Tim 2:11–15 and 1 Cor 14:34–35 are often cited to restrict women's leadership. However, these passages must be understood as context-specific instructions reflecting post-fall cultural accommodations within early institutional settings, not universal mandates for the *ekklesia*. In 1 Tim 2:11–15, Paul addresses situational concerns in Ephesus, likely countering false teaching tied to local myths, rather than prescribing eternal gender hierarchies. Similarly, 1 Cor 14:34–35 appears to regulate orderly worship in a chaotic Corinthian assembly, possibly as a quotation from opponents that Paul refutes, emphasizing decorum over prohibition. In the *ekklesia*, where oneness prevails (Gal 3:28), such texts do not override the Spirit's manifestations, which empower both men and women without distinction.

The fight for institutional inclusion simply affirms the pretext(s)—church and subordination (Gen 3:16)—over the truth, the *ekklesia* and fallen man's inclination.

ADDITIONAL REFERENCES AND CITATIONS

This perspective aligns with egalitarian critiques of institutional patriarchy as human distortions, though it prioritizes oneness over equality debates. For instance, egalitarian theologian Marg Mowczko notes that Paul used identical ministry terms for men and women, reflecting spiritual unity beyond gender restrictions.[9] Similarly, Mimi Haddad

---

9. Mowczko, *Beyond Authority*, 112.

highlights Christ's new creation as transcending patriarchal traditions.[10] Douglas Groothuis affirms that no biblical text eternally restricts women from leadership.[11] Diana Butler Bass critiques hierarchical systems as inherently oppressive.[12] These views contrast with this book's emphasis on oneness as the divine ideal, independent of scholarly consensus.

CONCLUSION

This chapter advances a novel theological framework that distinguishes sharply between the institutional church—as a hierarchical, temporal organization shaped by human traditions—and the *ekklesia*—as an organic, eternal body of Christ unified by the Spirit. The author's unique contribution lies in reinterpreting pre-fall complementarity (Gen 2:18–25) as the divine ideal of mutual completion, rendering equality a by-product of sin's distortion (Gen 3:16), where the woman's "desire" reflects a longing for restoration met by male dominance. This shifts the ordination debate from equality to oneness (e.g., Gal 3:28; 1 Cor 12), empowering women in ministry without institutional pretexts like ordination, which originated in translation biases (e.g., Tyndale's influence). By addressing countertexts contextually and prioritizing Spirit-led unity over patriarchal structures, the work critiques both egalitarian and complementarian views, offering a biblically grounded path that transcends post-fall hierarchies for organic service in the *ekklesia*.

---

10. Haddad, "Egalitarianism," 3–9.
11. Pierce, *Discovering Biblical Equality*, 98–110.
12. Bass, *Freeing Jesus*, 145–60.

13

The Spiritual Gifts Fallacy
A Contextual and Lexical Reconsideration of 1 Corinthians 12

THE MISINTERPRETATION OF 1 Cor 12 as a catalog of spiritual gifts represents one of the most persistent translation and theological errors in Christian doctrine. Many modern Christian traditions are built upon a doctrinal understanding of spiritual gifts drawn chiefly from 1 Cor 12 and Rom 12. However, a careful exegesis of these texts, particularly 1 Cor 12, reveals serious linguistic and contextual problems with the notion of spiritual gifts as commonly understood. This chapter aims to reevaluate the relevant terms—πνευματικῶν (*pneumatikōn*) and χαρισμάτων (*charismatōn*)—within their grammatical, historical, and theological contexts, challenging the legacy of translation errors and recovering the apostle Paul's original focus: not on "gifts" as possessions, but on Spirit-initiated manifestations distributed for the *ekklesia*. This analysis contrasts these with the more clearly articulated concept of gifts in Eph 4.

THE GREEK TERMS IN CONTEXT

The opening verse of 1 Cor 12 reads in Greek: Περὶ δὲ τῶν πνευματικῶν, ἀδελφοί, οὐ θέλω ὑμᾶς ἀγνοεῖν. Most English translations render πνευματικῶν as "spiritual gifts," yet this term is a genitive plural of πνευματικός (*pneumatikos*), meaning "spiritual," and lacks a specific noun. The term could be masculine ("spiritual persons") or neuter ("spiritual things"). There is no justification in the grammar for inserting "gifts," as neither δῶρον (*dōron*) nor δόμα (*doma*) appears in verse 1.[1] The phrase πνευματικῶν is a neuter plural adjective functioning substantively, often rendered "spiritual things" or "spiritual matters."[2] Early English translations, such as the Wycliffe Bible (1382), render it: "But of spiritual things, brethren, I will not, that ye unknowe," and William Tyndale (1526) similarly translates: "In spiritual thynges brethren I wolde not haue you ignoraut."[3]

Paul's actual referent is clarified in verse 7: ἑκάστῳ δὲ δίδοται ἡ φανέρωσις τοῦ πνεύματος πρὸς τὸ συμφέρον—"But to each one is given the manifestation of the Spirit for the common good" (1 Cor 12:7). This verse is the key to understanding Paul's argument: he is referring to momentary, Spirit-initiated manifestations, not permanent possessions or individual talents. The term φανέρωσις (*phanerōsis*), meaning "disclosure" or "manifestation," underscores the transient, divine action of the Spirit, as seen in 2 Cor 4:2, where Paul uses it to describe the open proclamation of truth.[4]

The subsequent verses (vv. 8–10) list these manifestations: λόγος σοφίας (word of wisdom), λόγος γνώσεως (word of knowledge), πίστις (faith), ἰάματα (healings), ἐνεργήματα δυνάμεων (workings of miracles), προφητεία (prophecy), and so on. These are not "gifts" people own or control; they are acts of the Spirit, distributed "as He wills" (1 Cor 12:11). This emphasis on divine sovereignty aligns with 1 Cor 12:18, where Paul stresses that God arranges the body's members as he chooses.

The Greek term χαρισμάτων (*charismatōn*) in verse 4, derived from χάρις (grace), also does not imply possession. It describes divine favor or operations of grace. The focus is on what is given, not what is owned. N. T. Wright reinforces this, noting that *charismata* are "concrete instances of grace at work," not personal endowments.[5] Tyndale's translation of 1 Cor

---

1. Fee, *First Epistle*, 576.
2. Bauer, *Greek-English Lexicon*, s.v. "πνευματικός."
3. Wycliffe, *Wycliffe Bible*, 1 Cor 12:1; Tyndale, *New Testament*, 1 Cor 12:1.
4. Thiselton, *First Epistle*, 930; Bauer, *Greek-English Lexicon*, s.v. "φανέρωσις."
5. Wright, *Paul and the Faithfulness*, 894.

12:4 as "There are diversities of gyftes verely, yet but one sprete" marks a turning point, introducing "gifts" for *charismata* and influencing later translations like the New American Standard Bible, which states, "Now there are varieties of gifts, but the same Spirit" (1 Cor 12:4).[6]

To clarify Paul's intent, the following terms are distinct in 1 Cor 12:

Greek Term	English Sense	Reference
πνευματικῶν	Spiritual manifestations	v. 1
φανέρωσις	Manifestation	v. 7
χαρίσματα	Gracious endowments	v. 4

Table 2

The primary controlling noun is φανέρωσις (v. 7), emphasizing that these manifestations originate from the Spirit, are dynamic operations, and are shared for the *ekklesia*'s good. A more accurate translation of 1 Cor 12:1–2 would be:

> Now concerning spiritual manifestations, brothers, I do not want you to be uninformed. You know that when you were gentiles, you were led astray to mute idols, however you were led.

THEOLOGICAL SUPPORT AND SCHOLARLY COMMENTARY

Gordon Fee writes,

> Paul is not speaking of gifts possessed but of the Spirit's activity in the body.[7]

Anthony Thiselton agrees, observing,

> Charismata are not talents or possessions, but manifestations in service to others.[8]

Craig Keener notes,

---

6. Tyndale, *New Testament*, 1 Cor 12:4.
7. Fee, *First Epistle*, 582.
8. Thiselton, *First Epistle*, 925.

Many readers anachronistically read modern concepts of spiritual gifts into Paul's words. Paul emphasizes God's sovereignty, not human ownership.⁹

Richard Hays adds that Paul's focus in 1 Cor 12 is on "the communal edification of the body," not individual empowerment.¹⁰ D. A. Carson reinforces this, stating that the Spirit's manifestations are "situation-specific, not permanent endowments."¹¹

These insights converge on one crucial point: the manifestations described by Paul in 1 Cor 12 are not "gifts" in the modern sense but are better understood as sovereign distributions of divine action. This aligns with Paul's broader theology of the Spirit, as seen in Gal 5:22–23, where the "fruit of the Spirit" (v. 22) similarly emphasizes divine work over human possession.

CONTRASTING EPHESIANS 4

Paul's use of "gifts" in Eph 4 is not arbitrary. It is rooted directly in the Septuagint (LXX) rendering of Ps 68:18, which reads:

> ἀνέβης εἰς ὕψος, ᾐχμαλώτευσας αἰχμαλωσίαν, ἔλαβες δόματα ἐν ἀνθρώπῳ (Ps 67:19 LXX); You have ascended on high, You have led captive Your captives; You have received gifts among men. (Ps 68:18)

Paul adapts this in Eph 4:8:

> Διὸ λέγει· ἀναβὰς εἰς ὕψος ᾐχμαλώτευσεν αἰχμαλωσίαν, καὶ ἔδωκεν δόματα τοῖς ἀνθρώποις; Therefore it says, "When He ascended on high, /He led captive the captives, / And He gave gifts to people." (Eph 4:8)

The LXX uses ἔλαβες δόματα (you received gifts), which Paul intentionally shifts to ἔδωκεν δόματα (he gave gifts), reinforcing Christ as the giver of people to the church.¹²

The key term here, δόματα (*domata*), is the noun explicitly meaning "gifts," and ἔδωκεν (*edōken*) is the aorist of δίδωμι ("to give"). Paul

---

9. Keener, *Gift and Giver*, 35.
10. Hays, *First Corinthians*, 209.
11. Carson, *Showing the Spirit*, 39.
12. Fee, *God's Empowering Presence*, 707.

intentionally quotes and modifies the LXX to highlight Christ as the Giver of actual gifts—namely, the persons given in Eph 4:11 (apostles, prophets, evangelists, pastors, and teachers).

This linguistic and theological grounding stands in sharp contrast to the insertion of "gifts" in 1 Cor 12 and Rom 12, where no such nouns appear in the key introductory verses. Instead, Paul uses terms such as πνευματικῶν ("spiritual things"), χαρισμάτων ("graces"), and φανέρωσις ("manifestation"), never δόματα. For example, Rom 12:6 uses χαρίσματα (*charismata*), emphasizing grace-enabled functions for the body's unity (Rom 12:4–5).

Ephesians 4:7–11 provides a clearer example of enduring, divinely appointed roles. Verse 8 quotes Ps 68:18 from the LXX:

> ἀνέβης εἰς ὕψος, ᾐχμαλώτευσας αἰχμαλωσίαν, ἔδωκας δόματα τοῖς ἀνθρώποις; When He ascended on high, / He led captive the captives, / And He gave gifts to people. (Eph 4:8)

The term here, δόματα (*domata*), literally means "gifts" and is a noun. In Eph 4:11, Christ gives people as gifts: "And He gave some as apostles, and some as prophets." The verb ἔδωκεν (*edōken*, "He gave") and the noun δόματα confirm the concept of actual divine gifts in the form of people for the edification of the church. This stands in contrast to 1 Cor 12, where no such terms or concepts of ownership appear.

The Eph 4 gifts are fixed, functional roles tied to the ongoing structure and leadership of the body. The manifestations in 1 Cor 12 are momentary and dependent upon the Spirit's will. As Fee notes, "Ephesians 4 speaks of Christ's gift of persons for ministry roles, while 1 Corinthians 12 emphasizes the Spirit's spontaneous activity."[13]

THEOLOGICAL IMPLICATIONS

The insistence on interpreting 1 Cor 12 as a catalog of spiritual gifts risks distorting Paul's message. Rather than promoting a theology of Spirit-led interdependence, it can promote spiritual consumerism and self-identification. This misreading has three damaging effects: it individualizes divine action, portraying manifestations as personal possessions; it breaks the contextual continuity between 1 Cor 12:1 and 12:7,

---

13. Fee, *God's Empowering Presence*, 707.

creating an artificial division in Paul's logic; and it fosters ecclesiological confusion, emphasizing individual giftedness over the common good *sumpheron*, (1 Cor 12:7). Paul's intent was to emphasize unity in diversity under the authority of the Spirit, as seen in 1 Cor 12:12–13, where the body's unity is likened to baptism in one Spirit, and 1 Cor 12:21–26, where no member can claim superiority.

The traditional language of "gifts" thus reflects a theological and translational error: one that has been canonized through uncritical repetition in lexicons, commentaries, and translations. By restoring Paul's focus on Spirit-initiated manifestations, the text regains its pneumatological integrity and ecclesial focus. As Carson notes, "Paul's concern is the Spirit's activity for the church's upbuilding, not the allocation of permanent gifts."[14]

UNDERSTANDING THE MANIFESTATIONS OF THE SPIRIT: THE IMPLICATIONS OF GRACES IN 1 CORINTHIANS 12-14

This section of the chapter reexamines the Pauline concept of "spiritual manifestations" (πνευματικῶν) in 1 Cor 12–14, arguing against the traditional "gifts" paradigm in favor of a dynamic, Spirit-initiated model. Central to this discussion is the phenomenon of "tongues" (γλῶσσαι), which, when understood as actual languages (as in Acts 2), reshapes charismatic theology. Drawing from lexical, historical, and theological analysis, this study contends that the Spirit's manifestations—including prophecy, healing, and tongues—are not personal endowments but sovereign acts of divine grace (χαρίσματα) for the church's edification.

The modern Pentecostal and charismatic movements have popularized the idea of spiritual gifts as personal, permanent abilities. However, a close reading of 1 Cor 12–14 reveals that Paul never describes these phenomena as "gifts" (δόματα) but as manifestations (φανέρωσις) of the Spirit (12:7). This section argues:

1. "Tongues" (γλῶσσαι) should be understood as human languages (as in Acts 2:4–11), not ecstatic speech.
2. The Spirit's manifestations are situational, not personal possessions.

---

14. Carson, *Showing the Spirit*, 40.

3. Paul's emphasis is on intelligibility and edification (1 Cor 14:1–19).

Lexical and Contextual Analysis

A. Πνευματικῶν (Pneumatikōn) as "Spiritual Manifestations"

> Περὶ δὲ τῶν πνευματικῶν, ἀδελφοί, οὐ θέλω ὑμᾶς ἀγνοεῖν.
> Now concerning spiritual gifts, brothers and sisters, I do not want you to be unaware. (1 Cor 12:1)

- πνευματικῶν is a substantival adjective ("spiritual things/manifestations"), not "gifts."[15]
- Early English translations (Wycliffe, Tyndale) rendered it "spiritual things," not "gifts."[16]

B. Φανέρωσις (Phanerōsis) as "Manifestation" (12:7)

> ἑκάστῳ δὲ δίδοται ἡ φανέρωσις τοῦ πνεύματος πρὸς τὸ συμφέρον.
> But to each one is given the manifestation of the Spirit for the common good. (1 Cor 12:7)

- φανέρωσις means "disclosure" or "appearance," emphasizing momentary, divine action, not human ability.

C. Γλῶσσαι (Glōssai) as "Languages" (Acts 2, 1 Cor 14)

- Acts 2:4–11 clearly describes tongues as known languages (διαλέκτοις, dialektois).
- 1 Cor 14:10–11 assumes tongues have linguistic structure ("none is incapable of meaning," v. 10).
- 1 Cor 14:21–22 quotes Isa 28:11, where foreign languages signify judgment—further supporting intelligibility.

---

15. Bauer, *Greek-English Lexicon*, s.v. "πνευματικός."
16. Tyndale, *New Testament*, 1 Cor 12:1.

The evidence suggests glossolalia in Acts and 1 Corinthians refers to actual languages, not ecstatic utterances.[17]

Theological Implications

A. The Spirit's Authority Over Human Control

- 1 Cor 12:11: "The Spirit apportions to each one individually as he wills."
- Not a "gift" to be claimed, but a manifestation to be received.

B. The Ecclesial Purpose of Manifestations

- 1 Cor 12:7: "For the common good."
- 1 Cor 14:26: "Let all things be done for building up."

C. Tongues in Worship: Intelligibility Over Mysticism

- Uninterpreted tongues do not edify (1 Cor 14:6–9).
- Prophecy is superior because it builds up the *ekklesia* (1 Cor 14:1–5).

CONCLUSION

Paul's theology in 1 Cor 12–14 emphasizes the Spirit's dynamic work, not static gifts. Tongues, when properly understood as languages, align with Acts 2 and reinforce Paul's insistence on intelligible worship. Churches must move beyond the "gifts" paradigm and embrace a pneumatological model—well suited for the first century *ekklesia*—where the Spirit's manifestations serve the body over the individual.

---

17. Keener, *Acts*, 820–23.

14

John 17:4–5
Eternity and Entropy

BIBLICAL AND THEOLOGICAL SUPPORT

THE INTERPRETATION PRESENTED IN this chapter, which posits that Jesus' pre-crucifixion glorification in John 17:4–5 is a completed work that enables believers to participate in eternal life by transcending entropy, finds significant support in biblical texts and theological traditions.[1] Below, I outline the key biblical and theological foundations that align with this interpretation, followed by an analysis of its unique contribution to Johannine scholarship.

1. Exegetical Foundations in John 17:4–5

The use of the aorist active participle *teleiōsas* ("having accomplished") in John 17:4 strongly supports the claim that Jesus had completed a specific work prior to the cross. This work, as elucidated in John 17:6–8, involves revealing the Father's name, imparting divine truth, and securing the disciples' faith. This is consistent with John's broader emphasis on Jesus as the divine Logos who reveals the Father. The request for

---

1. Frame, *Doctrine of God*, 428–31.

glorification in John 17:5, tied to the pre-incarnate glory Jesus shared with the Father, suggests a restoration to a state of divine incorruptibility.[2] This is consistent with John 1:1, which establishes Jesus' preexistent divine nature, and Phil 2:6–8, which describes the kenotic self-emptying that subjected Jesus to human limitations, including entropy.

2. Theological Support for Glorification and Entropy

The chapter's assertion that glorification enables believers to live bodily in eternity by overcoming entropy finds resonance in several biblical and theological sources:

- 2 Pet 1:4: The notion of believers becoming "partakers of the divine nature" directly supports the idea that glorification involves participation in a divine state free from corruption. This aligns with the chapter's claim that glorification transcends the second law of thermodynamics, which governs decay and entropy in the physical world.

- Rom 8:29–30 and 1 Cor 15:42–49: Paul's discussion of glorification and the resurrection body as "imperishable" and "spiritual" complements the Johannine perspective. While Paul emphasizes the future bodily resurrection, John's focus on Jesus' relational glorification through union with his Father (John 17:21–23) suggests a present participation in divine life that anticipates the eschatological state.

- John 5:26: Jesus declares, "For just as the Father has life in Himself, so He gave to the Son also to have life in Himself," affirming Christ's self-sustaining life that grants believers participation in entropy-transcending eternal life. Leon Morris notes that this verse underscores Jesus' authority to bestow eternal life, aligning with the chapter's thesis of glorification overcoming decay.[3]

- John 12:27–28: The Father's declaration, "I have both glorified it, and will glorify it again" (v. 28), supports the argument that glorification is not solely tied to the cross or resurrection but is a process initiated through Jesus' obedient life and revelatory mission. This

---

2. Brown, *Gospel According to John*, 742–45.
3. Morris, *Gospel According to John*, 270–72.

dual glorification (past and future) reinforces the idea that Jesus' pre-crucifixion work was a critical component of his glorification.

- Patristic theology: The writings of Athanasius and Gregory of Nyssa are apt to this chapter's argument. Athanasius argues that the incarnation restores humanity to incorruptibility through Christ's divine nature.[4] Similarly, Gregory of Nyssa emphasizes the resurrection as a restoration to a prelapsarian state free from decay.[5] These patristic insights provide theological grounding for the chapter's claim that glorification involves a transcendence of entropy, enabling eternal bodily existence.

3. Theological Coherence Across Johannine and Pauline Perspectives

The chapter adeptly addresses potential theological tensions between John and Paul by demonstrating their complementarity. John's emphasis on present relational glorification (John 17:22–24) and Paul's focus on future bodily glorification (Rom 8:29–30; 1 Cor 15:42–49) are not contradictory but represent different aspects of the same redemptive process. Some scholars, like Rudolf Schnackenburg, argue that John's glorification is primarily relational, focusing on spiritual union rather than physical transformation, but this perspective complements Paul's emphasis on bodily resurrection, as both address the transcendence of decay through divine life.[6] This synthesis strengthens the chapter's argument that Jesus' glorification initiates a transformative process that culminates in the eschatological glorification of believers.

4. Entropy and the Second Law of Thermodynamics

This Johannine-Pauline synthesis provides a foundation for exploring glorification's implications in physical terms, particularly through the lens of entropy and eternal life. The chapter's unique contribution lies in its application of the second law of thermodynamics to theological anthropology. The second law, which states that entropy (disorder) in a

---

4. Athanasius, *On the Incarnation*, 54–56.
5. Gregory of Nyssa, *On the Soul*, 439–40.
6. Schnackenburg, *Gospel*, 172–74.

closed system increases over time, is a fundamental principle of physical decay.[7] By proposing that Jesus' glorification reverses this entropic process, the chapter offers a novel theological framework for understanding eternal life as not merely unending but qualitatively divine and incorruptible. This aligns with Heb 5:8-9, which describes Jesus' obedience as the means by which he became the source of eternal salvation, and with John 17:2-3, where eternal life is defined as knowing the Father and the Son—a relational state that transcends physical decay.

Biblical support for this thesis is robust, portraying glorification as a divine reversal of entropy-like decay, enabling believers to partake in incorruptible, eternal life. In John 17:1-5, Jesus prays for glorification to grant eternal life to those the Father has given him, defining it as intimate knowledge of God (v. 3), which implies a restoration beyond temporal decay. Rom 8:18-23 depicts creation subjected to futility and decay (bondage to corruption, akin to entropy), groaning for redemption alongside believers, whose glorification liberates them from physical corruption through adoption and bodily redemption. First Corinthians 15:42-54 elaborates on this reversal: bodies sown perishable and in dishonor are raised imperishable and in glory, with mortality swallowed up by life, directly countering decay, as "the last enemy to be abolished is death" (v. 26). Philippians 3:20-21 affirms Christ's power to transform lowly bodies to conform to his glorious body, subduing all things—including entropic forces—to himself. Second Corinthians 4:16-18 contrasts the outer self wasting away (entropy) with the inner self renewed daily, oriented toward an eternal weight of glory beyond temporal affliction. Colossians 3:4 links glorification to Christ's revelation—"When Christ, who is our life, is revealed, then you also will be revealed with Him in glory"—implying a qualitative eternal existence free from decay. Revelation 21:4 promises no more death, mourning, or pain, with former things (including decay) passed away, portraying a renewed creation where entropy is nullified. Second Peter 3:13 promises new heavens and a new earth where righteousness dwells, implying a cosmic reversal of entropy's disorder.

While this thesis is novel, reputable scholars offer insights connecting glorification, eternal life, and concepts akin to entropy reversal, viewing life's victory over decay as a theological pointer to divine

---

7. Polkinghorne, *God of Hope*, 98-100.

renewal. N. T. Wright, in *Surprised by Hope*, argues that resurrection and glorification reverse creation's decay, transforming perishable bodies into imperishable ones (1 Cor 15), reflecting God's defeat of entropy-like futility in Rom 8, where creation awaits liberation from bondage to corruption.[8] John Polkinghorne, a physicist-theologian, in *The Faith of a Physicist*, posits that life's emergence against entropy foreshadows eschatological renewal, where glorification in Christ (Phil 3:21) reverses thermodynamic decay through divine energy, enabling eternal, incorruptible existence.[9] Alister McGrath, in *The Open Secret*, describes eternal life as qualitative participation in God's glory (John 17:24), transcending entropy's disorder through Christ's transformative power, aligning with Heb 5:9's eternal salvation as reversal of human fragility.[10] Jürgen Moltmann, in *The Coming of God*, views glorification as cosmic redemption from entropy, where eternal life (John 17:3) involves a new creation free from decay, grounded in Christ's resurrection as the inbreaking of divine order.[11] This application uses entropy metaphorically to illuminate theological truths, not as empirical proof, aligning with Polkinghorne's integration of physics and eschatology.[12]

UNIQUE CONTRIBUTION TO JOHANNINE SCHOLARSHIP

The chapter's interpretation of John 17:4–5 makes a significant and original contribution to the literature by integrating theological, exegetical, and scientific perspectives in the following ways:

1. Pre-crucifixion glorification: While many scholars focus on the cross and resurrection as the locus of Jesus' glorification, this chapter argues that Jesus' revelatory and preparatory work among the disciples constitutes a completed act of glorification prior to the cross. This perspective challenges traditional interpretations and highlights the significance of Jesus' earthly ministry as a glorifying act in itself.

---

8. Wright, *Surprised by Hope*, 160–62.
9. Polkinghorne, *Faith of a Physicist*, 148–50.
10. McGrath, *Open Secret*, 238–40.
11. Moltmann, *Coming of God*, 234–36.
12. Polkinghorne, *Faith of a Physicist*, 148–50.

2. Entropy and eternal life: The chapter's proposal that glorification involves the transcendence of entropy is a groundbreaking theological-scientific synthesis. By framing eternal life as a state free from the second law of thermodynamics, the chapter bridges biblical theology with contemporary scientific paradigms, a move that resonates with the work of theologians like John Polkinghorne.

3. Relational and eschatological unity: The chapter's emphasis on the unity prayed for in John 17:21–23 as a "pre-entropic state" shared with the Father and Son is a novel contribution. While scholars like T. F. Torrance emphasize the relational aspect of John 17, this chapter uniquely ties this unity to the physical and metaphysical implications of glorification.[13]

4. Practical implications for mission: By connecting Jesus' glorification to the empowerment of disciples for mission (John 17:18, 23), the chapter underscores the practical outworking of glorification. This perspective enriches the theological understanding of eternal life as a transformative reality that manifests in the present through the church's witness

RESPONSES TO POTENTIAL CHALLENGES

The chapter effectively anticipates and addresses the following theological and philosophical objections:

- Glorification is tied to the cross and resurrection: The chapter acknowledges the centrality of the cross while arguing that John's perspective highlights a distinct pre-crucifixion work. This is supported by the Father's affirmation in John 12:28 and the completed actions described in John 17:6–8.

- John contradicts Paul: The chapter reconciles these perspectives by showing that John's relational glorification complements Paul's eschatological focus, a synthesis that aligns with patristic and modern theological insights.

---

13. For T. F. Torrance's extensive work on the relational and ontological unity articulated in John 17, see his *Trinitarian Faith*, 49–50 and 308–310, where he explores the perichoretic (mutually indwelling) unity between the Father and the Son as the ground of all theological and ecclesial reality.

- Entropy as a theological category: While the application of the second law of thermodynamics is unconventional, it is grounded in the biblical concept of incorruptibility and patristic teachings on divine participation.

CONCLUSION

Theological Synthesis

The interpretation of John 17:4–5 presented in this chapter offers a robust synthesis of Johannine theology, integrating Jesus' pre-crucifixion glorification with a novel theological-scientific framework. By positing that glorification reverses entropy, enabling believers to participate in eternal life, the chapter aligns with biblical texts like John 17:1–5, Rom 8:18–23, and 1 Cor 15:42–54, which depict eternal life as a divine, incorruptible state free from decay. The complementarity of John's relational focus and Paul's eschatological vision, supported by patristic insights from Athanasius and Gregory of Nyssa, underscores the coherence of this view, bridging present and future dimensions of glorification.

Interdisciplinary Contribution

The chapter's unique contribution lies in its application of the second law of thermodynamics to theological anthropology, framing eternal life as a qualitative transcendence of entropy's disorder. Scholars like N. T. Wright, John Polkinghorne, Alister McGrath, and Jürgen Moltmann provide theological grounding, viewing glorification as a reversal of entropy, aligning with texts like Phil 3:20–21 and Rev 21:4. This interdisciplinary approach challenges traditional readings, offering a fresh lens for understanding eternal life as both relational and physically transformative, resonant with contemporary scientific paradigms.

Practical Implications

By connecting Jesus' glorification to the disciples' mission (John 17:18, 23), the chapter emphasizes that eternal life begins in the present, empowering the church's witness through participation in Christ's glory.

This perspective invites believers to embody a pre-entropic state of unity and divine life, fostering a lived theology that counters decay through relational and missional engagement.

Future Research Directions

This interpretation opens avenues for further exploration, particularly in eschatological ecology, linking the vision of glorification in John 17 to the renewed creation in Rev 21, where entropy is nullified. Future studies could investigate how the concept of entropy reversal applies to broader ecological and cosmic redemption, integrating insights from theology and science to deepen our understanding of eternal life as a transformative reality.

15

The Hiddenness of God

THE PROBLEM OF THE hiddenness of God, often raised in Christian apologetics, posits that if God exists, his presence should be empirically undeniable. This critique, however, rests on a flawed materialist assumption that limits reality to what can be observed and measured through sensory experience. This chapter argues that God's apparent hiddenness is not a divine failing but a consequence of employing inadequate materialist methods to apprehend a spiritual God. The chapter offers a refined perspective on divine hiddenness, arguing that the absence of faith is what makes it appear that God is hidden, since faith is the only way to apprehend spiritual realities. Engaging Deut 29 and Isa 45, the author balances philosophical challenges with theological assurance, framing hiddenness as purposeful for fostering faith and moral growth. While theological literature addresses hiddenness as potentially receiver-dependent due to lack of faith, this nuanced application enriches apologetics by emphasizing faith as the essential mechanism for perceiving divine presence amid mystery. By adopting faith as an epistemic tool, as articulated in Scripture and supported by theological and philosophical traditions, one can perceive God's presence clearly, exposing the hiddenness argument as a misapplication of epistemology. This perspective is further expanded through an in-depth exploration

THE HIDDENNESS OF GOD

of belief and faith's inseparability, demonstrating how faith undergirds all apprehension of divine reality.

THE MATERIALIST ASSUMPTION DEFINED

Materialism, rooted in Enlightenment philosophy (e.g., David Hume's empiricism and John Locke's sensory epistemology), assumes that only physical phenomena, accessible through observation, experimentation, and quantification, constitute reality.[1] This perspective, exemplified by logical positivism's demand for verifiable evidence, dismisses nonempirical realities such as the spiritual.[2] Consequently, materialism seeks God through scientific methods—e.g., repeatable experiments or sensory detection—methods inherently unsuited to apprehending a nonphysical, transcendent, and personal being. As Immanuel Kant argued in *Critique of Pure Reason*, human perception is limited to phenomena (things as they appear), leaving noumenal realities like God beyond empirical reach.[3] Materialism's assumption thus creates a self-fulfilling prophecy: by rejecting non-sensory epistemologies, it ensures God remains "hidden."

FAITH AS AN EPISTEMIC TOOL

Faith, far from being blind or irrational, serves as a distinct epistemic faculty for apprehending spiritual realities. Hebrews 11:1 defines it as "the certainty of things hoped for, a proof of things not seen." This verse establishes faith as a confident trust in divine revelation, enabling believers to perceive truths beyond physical sight. Faith operates through divine illumination, where God's Spirit reveals his presence and truth to the believer (John 16:13). It is not mere wishful thinking but a rational response to God's self-disclosure in creation, Scripture, and conscience. Augustine's maxim, "I believe in order that I may understand," underscores that faith precedes and enables spiritual understanding, a principle echoed by Alvin Plantinga's reformed epistemology, which

---

1. Hume, *Enquiry Concerning Human Understanding*, 101–20.
2. Locke, *Essay Concerning Human Understanding*, bk. 2, ch. 1, sec. 1–5 (104–08).
3. Kant, *Critique of Pure Reason*, B294–B315.

posits belief in God as "properly basic."[4] Unlike materialism's reliance on sensory data, faith engages the heart and mind holistically, aligning with God's spiritual nature:

> "God is spirit, and those who worship Him must worship in spirit and truth." (John 4:24)

John Calvin, in his *Institutes of the Christian Religion*, articulates the concept of *sensus divinitatis*, an innate sense of divinity implanted in all humans, making knowledge of God instinctive and inexcusable to suppress.[5] This aligns with Rom 1:19–20, suggesting that even agnostics or atheists suppress an inherent faith, distorted by sin's "disease." Plantinga's *Warranted Christian Belief* argues that belief in God can be "properly basic," akin to sensory or memory-based beliefs, grounded in the faith allotted by God (Rom 12:3).[6] Karl Barth, while critical of natural theology, affirms in *Church Dogmatics* that humanity's rejection of God presupposes prior awareness, aligning with Rom 1:21's "futile reasoning."[7]

ADDRESSING COUNTERARGUMENTS: SUBJECTIVE AND CORPORATE FAITH

Critics of faith often argue that it is subjective, varying by individual and thus unreliable. While faith involves personal conviction, Scripture affirms its objective grounding in God's revelation. Rom 10:17 states, "So faith comes from hearing, and hearing by the word of Christ," indicating that faith is rooted in the objective truth of Scripture, not merely personal feelings. Furthermore, faith is not solely individualistic but corporate, sustained within the community of believers. Hebrews 10:24–25 encourages believers to "consider how to stimulate one another to love and good deeds, not forsaking our own assembling together," highlighting the communal reinforcement of faith. The corporate nature of faith, exemplified in the early *ekklesia* (Acts 2:42–44), counters the charge of

---

4. Augustine, *On Free Choice*, 1.2 (6); Plantinga, *Warranted Christian Belief*, 167–98.
5. Calvin, *Institutes*, 1.3.1–3.
6. Plantinga, *Warranted Christian Belief*, 167–98.
7. Barth, *Church Dogmatics*, 3/1, 121–28.

THE HIDDENNESS OF GOD

subjectivity by rooting belief in shared testimony and practice, providing a robust framework for apprehending God's presence.

BIBLICAL EVIDENCE EXPOSING MATERIALIST PERSPECTIVES

Scripture consistently affirms that God's presence is evident through faith, exposing materialism's limitations. The following passages, contextualized and integrated, illustrate this.

1. Romans 1:20: In Rom 1, Paul addresses gentile idolatry, arguing that God's existence is evident despite human rebellion.

   > For since the creation of the world His invisible attributes, that is, His eternal power and divine nature, have been clearly perceived, being understood by what has been made, so that they are without excuse.

   Materialism's empirical demands fail to perceive these "invisible attributes," as it seeks physical proof for a nonphysical God, ignoring creation's testimony. This passage elaborates,

   > For the wrath of God is revealed from heaven against all ungodliness and unrighteousness of people who suppress the truth in unrighteousness, because that which is known about God is evident within them; for God made it evident to them. (Rom 1:18–23)

2. Hebrews 11:3: Hebrews 11 catalogs heroes of faith, emphasizing faith's role in understanding divine truths.

   > By faith we understand that the world has been created by the word of God so that what is seen has not been made out of things that are visible.

   Materialism, reliant on visible causes, cannot account for creation's spiritual origin, rendering it blind to God's creative power.

3. Colossians 1:15–17: In Colossians, Paul counters false teachings by affirming Christ's supremacy.

   > He is the image of the invisible God, the firstborn of all creation: for by Him all things were created, both in the heavens and on earth, visible and invisible ... all things have been created through

Him and for Him. He is before all things, and in Him all things hold together.

Materialism's focus on the visible ignores Christ's role as the mediator of both visible and invisible realities, accessible only through faith.

4. Romans 2:14–15: Within Paul's discussion of universal judgment, he notes,

> For when Gentiles who do not have the Law instinctively perform the requirements of the Law, these, though not having the Law, are a law to themselves, in that they show the work of the Law written in their hearts.

Materialism dismisses this moral intuition, seeking objective morality in physical processes, yet this passage reveals a spiritual law inscribed by God, perceptible through conscience.

5. John 4:24: In Christ's dialogue with the Samaritan woman, he declares,

> "God is spirit, and those who worship Him must worship in spirit and truth."

Materialism's sensory methods cannot engage a spiritual God, as worship requires a faith-informed approach aligned with his nature.

6. 2 Corinthians 4:3–4: Addressing the Corinthian church, Paul explains resistance to the gospel:

> And even if our gospel is veiled, it is veiled to those who are perishing, in whose case the god of this world has blinded the minds of the unbelieving so that they will not see the light of the gospel of the glory of Christ, who is the image of God.

Materialism, akin to the "god of this world," blinds adherents by prioritizing human reason over divine revelation, ensuring God's apparent hiddenness.

7. Romans 12:3:

> For through the grace given to me I say to everyone among you not to think more highly of himself than he ought to think; but to think so as to have sound judgment, as God has allotted to each a measure of faith.

This verse underscores that faith is not a privilege reserved for believers but a universal endowment, enabling belief in varying degrees across all human experience.

8. Psalm 19:1–2:

   The heavens tell of the glory of God;
   And their expanse declares the work of His hands.
   Day to day pours forth speech,
   And night to night reveals knowledge.

   This external revelation, accessible to all, complements Rom 1:20, yet sinful distortion obscures it partially, retaining accountability.

9. Acts 17:22–31: Paul notes that God "is not far from each one of us" (v. 27), supporting the internal evidence of God and critiquing idolatrous suppression.

10. Ephesians 2:8–9:

    For by grace you have been saved through faith; and this is not of yourselves, it is the gift of God; not a result of works, so that no one may boast.

    This reinforces faith as a divine gift enabling all belief, though its salvific application requires response.

PHILOSOPHICAL ECHOES

Philosophical perspectives reinforce the inseparability of belief and faith, challenging hierarchies that deem faith irrational. Ludwig Wittgenstein's *On Certainty* describes "hinge propositions"—unquestioned beliefs enabling inquiry—as faith-like commitments.[8] For example, belief in the reliability of perception underpins scientific inquiry, paralleling the faith in Rom 12:3. Michael Polanyi's *Personal Knowledge* posits that scientific discovery involves "fiduciary" acts of trust in community norms and judgment.[9] This counters secular dismissals of faith, showing empirical beliefs as faith-oriented, distorted by sin when misdirected. Paul Tillich's *Dynamics of Faith* defines faith as "ultimate concern," encompassing even nontheistic commitments like agnosticism's

---

8. Wittgenstein, *On Certainty*, §115–16.
9. Polanyi, *Personal Knowledge*, 266–68.

uncertainty.[10] Søren Kierkegaard's *Fear and Trembling* presents faith as a rational "leap" toward existential certainty, necessary for all belief.[11]

Philosopher	Key Concept	Relevance to Thesis
Wittgenstein	Hinge propositions	Shared commitments make belief intelligible, implying faith.
Polanyi	Personal knowledge	Scientific beliefs rely on fiduciary acts, akin to faith.
Tillich	Ultimate concern	Beliefs structure around commitments, even nontheistic ones.
Kierkegaard	Leap of faith	Faith as essential for existential belief, inescapable.

Table 3

THE LIMITATIONS OF MATERIALIST METHODS: AN ENHANCED ANALOGY

Materialism's methods—scientific empiricism, logical positivism, and reductionism—are like using a thermometer to measure sound, a ruler to weigh fruit, or a microscope to detect love. Scientific empiricism, which demands repeatable experiments, fails to capture God's transcendent nature, as he is not a phenomenon subject to laboratory conditions. Logical positivism, insisting on verifiable propositions, dismisses spiritual truths as "meaningless" because they lack sensory confirmation.[12] Reductionism, which reduces reality to physical components, cannot account for nonmaterial realities like purpose or morality. Just as one cannot measure a symphony's beauty with a voltmeter, materialism's tools are categorically misaligned with spiritual inquiry, ensuring God's apparent hiddenness by methodological design.

---

10. Tillich, *Dynamics of Faith*, 1–12.
11. Kierkegaard, *Fear and Trembling*, 46–53.
12. Ayer, *Language*, 114–20.

BELIEF AND FAITH: THE EPISTEMIC KEY TO UNVEILING DIVINE PRESENCE

The interplay between belief and faith constitutes a foundational aspect of human existence, meaning that all belief inherently requires faith, a principle rooted in biblical revelation and echoed in philosophical discourse. This section contends that faith is inescapable, even in secular or skeptical worldviews such as agnosticism, and that the Bible, through texts like Rom 12:3, Rom 1:18–23, and Heb 11:3, establishes this as normative. However, human sensibilities, distorted by sin, obscure these plain truths in some measure, yet not to the extent of excusing denial of God's evident reality. This argument challenges the traditional dichotomy between rational and faith-based epistemologies, advocating for epistemic humility while upholding scriptural authority, thereby directly addressing divine hiddenness as a product of suppressed faith.

ADDRESSING COUNTERARGUMENTS

Critics challenge three key ideas: first, that religious belief is fundamentally a matter of faith; second, that agnosticism constitutes its own form of faith; and third, that biblical texts can be used to prove all people inherently know God, even if that knowledge is distorted by sin. Below, major objections are addressed, integrating theological, biblical, and philosophical responses.

- **Faith as distinct and irrational**

Critics like Richard Dawkins, Sam Harris, and David Hume argue that belief can be evidence-based, rendering faith (trust without evidence) unnecessary and irrational.[13] This confuses the means (evidence) with the phenomenon of belief, which inherently involves commitment. If critics believe their claims, they exercise faith in their reasoning's reliability, as Polanyi's fiduciary acts suggest.[14] John 1:1–3,

---

13. Dawkins, *God Delusion*, 31–50; Harris, *End of Faith*, 65–72; Hume, *Dialogues Concerning Natural Religion*, 55–60.

14. Polanyi, *Personal Knowledge*, 264–68. Polanyi argues that all knowing relies on a "fiduciary act," a personal commitment to a framework of beliefs that we trust and from which we operate. This concept provides a philosophical foundation for the trust in divine revelation articulated in John 1:1–3.

"In the beginning was the Word.... All things came into being through Him," connects creation's evidence to Christ, showing faith as rational engagement with divine revelation.

- **Agnosticism and atheism as non-faith positions**

Thomas Huxley and Matt Dillahunty claim agnosticism and atheism involve no faith, only evidential restraint or lack of belief.[15] Declaring uncertainty, however, is a commitment to a position, violating noncontradiction if it denies its own belief status. Romans 12:3's universal faith measure implies even skepticism rests on faith in uncertainty's validity, distorted by sin's suppression (Rom 1:21).

- **Critiques of Romans 1's natural theology**

Karl Barth and Richard Hays question Rom 1:18-23's universal applicability, arguing true knowledge requires special revelation (Christ) or that global unbelief disproves evident truth.[16] Yet, John 1:1-3 aligns God's creative revelation with Christ, rendering "special revelation" redundant; creation itself reveals the Creator. Global unbelief illustrates the point made in Rom 1: suppression distorts evident truth in some measure, not wholly, preserving accountability (v. 20).[14]

- **Faith as undebatable or illogical**

Critics like Bertrand Russell assert faith resists logical scrutiny, unlike evidence-based belief.[17] If they believe this, they commit to a faith in logic's supremacy, qualifying faith by type rather than phenomenon. Plantinga's "properly basic" beliefs show faith's rationality,[18] and observable transformations in believers' behavior (e.g., Gal 5:22-23's fruits of the Spirit) provide falsifiable evidence, countering Karl Popper's falsifiability critique.[19]

---

15. Huxley, *Collected Essays*, 237-39.
16. Barth, *Church Dogmatics*, 2/1, 94-99; Hays, *Moral Vision*, 387-89.
17. Russell, *Why I Am Not*, 5-16.
18. Plantinga's *Warranted Christian Belief*, 167-98, develops the concept of "properly basic" beliefs to establish the intrinsic rationality of theistic faith. For Karl Popper's principle of falsifiability as a criterion for scientific theories, which this perspective challenges, see Popper, *Conjectures and Refutations*, 48-62.
19. Popper, *Logic of Scientific Discovery*, 40-42.

PRACTICAL IMPLICATIONS

Recognizing the interdependence of belief and faith reframes secular and religious discourses. Secular paradigms need not dismiss faith as irrational, as all inquiry rests on faith-based commitments. Religious apologetics can present belief as rational commitment, avoiding compromise while fostering dialogue. This dismantles the reason/faith binary, promoting epistemic humility without sacrificing biblical rigor. The partial obscuring of truth by sin explains apparent divine hiddenness while upholding human accountability, as God's revelation remains clear (Rom 1:20).

WHY IT MATTERS

On what basis would the psalmist declare that "the fool has said in his heart, 'There is no God'" (Ps 14:1)? This assertion is made in the context of the covenant community, where redemptive history attests to their survival and existence. A denial of Elohim, the Creator, Redeemer, Sustainer, is a rejection of the very breath and cognition that gave rise to the denial. The "fool" is therefore an appropriate identifier of the offender, who is a product of a social culture where denial is not an option. Their denial is in opposition to all that they are capable of knowing.

In what sense, if any, can this be applied generally to humanity? Redemptive history attests no less to the survival and existence of humanity. The apostle Paul observed, quoting the Greek poet, "In Him we live and move and exist" (Acts 17:28); and even if "the god" was unknown, those gathered at Mars Hill understood what it meant to live, move, and have their being; they simply had the wrong god, yet did not remotely imply that there was no God. Perhaps this is why Jesus discouraged calling anyone a fool (Matt 5:22). Fools represent those who enjoy the benefits of life yet deny its source. They represent those who ignore the obvious in favor of something about which they have no knowledge. In denying the source, they are ungrateful, and denial and ingratitude expose them as fools.

MEASURING TWICE, CUTTING ONCE

THE MISUSE OF "FOOL" IN CHRISTIAN APOLOGETICS

A minority of Christian apologists, citing Ps 14:1 and 53:1, may be tempted to label atheists as "fools," adopting a harsh tone that misaligns with Jesus' teachings in Matt 5:22. A better interpretation requires a nuanced understanding of the biblical "fool" as one who rejects God's covenantal wisdom, as seen in Matt 23:17 and Luke 12:16–21. These Psalms declare,

> The fool has said in his heart, "There is no God."
> They are corrupt, they have committed detestable acts;
> There is no one who does good. (Ps 14:1)[20]

Such a condemnation betrays the ethos of the New Testament, particularly Jesus' instruction in the Sermon on the Mount:

> "But I say to you that everyone who is angry with his brother shall be answerable to the court; and whoever says to his brother, 'You good-for-nothing,' shall be answerable to the supreme court; and whoever says, 'You fool,' shall be guilty enough to go into the fiery hell." (Matt 5:22)

A TEXT WITHOUT A CONTEXT IS A PRETEXT

The apparent tension between Jesus' prohibition on calling others "fool" (Matt 5:22) and his use of the term in Matt 23:17, alongside God's designation of the rich man as a "fool" in Luke 12:16–21, requires contextual analysis. Matthew 23 is pivotal in understanding Jesus' intent:

> "But woe to you, scribes and Pharisees, hypocrites, because you shut the kingdom of heaven in front of people; for you do not enter it yourselves, nor do you allow those who are entering to go in. Woe to you, scribes and Pharisees, hypocrites, because you travel around on sea and land to make one proselyte; and when he becomes one, you make him twice as much a son of hell as yourselves. Woe to you, blind guides, who say, 'Whoever swears by the temple, that is nothing; but whoever swears by the gold of the temple is obligated.' You fools and blind men! Which is more important, the gold or the temple that sanctified the gold?" (Matt 23:13–17)

---

20. "The fool has said in his heart, 'There is no God.' They are corrupt, and have committed abominable injustice; There is no one who does good" (Ps 53:1).

Jesus uses "fool" only once in Matt 23, alongside "blind" four times (vv. 17, 19, 24, 26), suggesting synonymity. His use of "fool," reflecting his divine authority as the revealer of God's truth (John 1:18), targets the scribes and Pharisees' willful rejection of covenantal wisdom and is not personal insult, distinguishing it from the interpersonal condemnation prohibited in Matt 5:22. To understand this usage, we turn to Ps 14:1 and 53:1, which provide the covenantal context for his critique.

PSALM 14:1 AND 53:1 IN CONTEXT

Ps 14:1 and 53:1 state,

> The fool has said in his heart, "There is no God."
> They are corrupt, they have committed detestable acts;
> There is no one who does good. (Ps 14:1)[21]

The Hebrew verb *hitibu* (הִתְעִיבוּ), meaning "they have caused an abomination" in its third-person plural form, indicates that the fool's denial of God disrupts the covenant community.[22] This mirrors the scribes and Pharisees' actions in Matt 23:13–15, where they block access to God's kingdom and lead proselytes astray, embodying the "detestable acts" condemned in the Psalms.[42] In Israel's theocracy, where children memorized God's laws and history (Deut 6:6–9; 7:18–22), denying YHWH amidst overwhelming evidence of his deliverance was a profound rejection of covenantal identity, marking one as a fool.

BIBLICAL DEFINITIONS OF A FOOL

The biblical "fool" transcends mere stupidity, encompassing spiritual, moral, and judgmental failures. Prov 10:14 states, "Wise people store up knowledge, but with the mouth of the foolish, ruin is at hand," paralleling the scribes and Pharisees' reckless teachings in Matt 23:16–17, which lead others to ruin. Similarly, Prov 13:16 notes, "Every prudent person acts with knowledge, but a fool displays foolishness," highlighting the fool's lack of discernment and unteachability, traits evident in

---

21. "The fool has said in his heart, 'There is no God.' They are corrupt, and have committed abominable injustice; There is no one who does good" (Ps 53:1).

22. Brown et al., *Hebrew and English Lexicon*, 1906, 1072.

the Pharisees' hypocrisy. This contrasts with modern apologists' use of "fool" to broadly condemn unbelievers, ignoring the biblical focus on covenantal unfaithfulness.

A BIBLICAL EXAMPLE OF A FOOL

The narrative of Nabal in 1 Sam 25 exemplifies the biblical fool, whose actions imperil others. Nabal (נָבָל, "fool") displays careless ingratitude and disrespect toward David, whose men protected Nabal's flocks, imperiling his entire household by provoking David's wrath, a consequence averted only by Abigail's intervention (1 Sam 25:23–35). Similarly, the scribes and Pharisees, by shutting the kingdom of heaven and making proselytes "twice as much a son of hell" (Matt 23:15), imperil the spiritual lives of others, embodying the "detestable acts" (*hitibu*) condemned in Ps 14:1 and 53:1. Likewise, the rich man's self-reliant hoarding in Luke 12:16–21, ignoring God's provision and the needs of others, reflects a foolishness that deprives the community, aligning with Jesus' critique of actions that endanger others. Nabal's foolishness, like that of the scribes and Pharisees, imperils others through covenantal unfaithfulness. This contrasts with modern apologists' misapplication of "fool" to dismiss unbelievers without addressing their potential to harm the spiritual community, contrary to Jesus' relational approach exemplified in his dialogue with the Samaritan woman (John 4:7–26). This emphasis on the fool's actions imperiling others, rooted in biblical examples, underscores the need for a nuanced apologetic approach in today's pluralistic context, where diverse worldviews demand discernment over condemnation.

MODERN CONTEXT AND APOLOGETIC IMPLICATIONS

Unlike Israel's theocratic context, where denying God was a rejection of covenantal identity (Ps 14:1; 53:1), today's pluralistic world features diverse worldviews, requiring a nuanced understanding of accountability.[40] A fool is not simply an unbeliever but one who willfully rejects God's wisdom, harming the covenant community, as seen in Nabal, the scribes and Pharisees, and the rich man. While some apologists may argue that Jesus' use of "fool" in Matt 23:17 justifies harsh rhetoric, his divine authority and focus on covenantal unfaithfulness distinguish his usage from broad condemnations of unbelievers in today's diverse context. Instead, apologists should reflect Jesus' relational engagement (Matt 5:22; John 4:7–26), adopting a posture of grace and discernment to invite dialogue rather than division, fostering understanding in a pluralistic world.

CONCLUSIONS

The argument for God's hiddenness stems from a methodological misstep: applying materialist tools, such as scientific empiricism and logical positivism, to apprehend a spiritual God. This is akin to the inadequacy of measuring a symphony's beauty with a voltmeter, as materialist methods are misaligned with spiritual inquiry.

Scripture counters this by affirming that God's presence is evident through faith, which serves as the epistemic key to perceiving divine realities. Passages like Rom 1:18–23, Heb 11:3, and Col 1:15–17 reveal that creation, conscience, and Christ's mediation make God's attributes accessible, yet sin's distortion obscures this truth, preserving human accountability. Deuteronomy 29:29 underscores that God's revelation is sufficient for faith, while Isa 45:15 acknowledges his mystery, yet faith unveils his presence.

Theological traditions and philosophical perspectives further support this view. Augustine, Calvin, and Plantinga, alongside Wittgenstein, Polanyi, Tillich, and Kierkegaard, reinforce that all belief rests on faith, challenging the reason/faith binary and exposing materialism's limitations.

The misuse of "fool" in apologetics, as seen in the misapplication of Ps 14:1 and 53:1, illustrates this epistemological error. Condemning unbelievers as fools without acknowledging the biblical fool's covenantal unfaithfulness and harm to others, as exemplified by Nabal, the scribes and Pharisees, and the rich man, perpetuates a harsh rhetoric misaligned with Jesus' teachings.

This relational approach, rooted in faith, contrasts with materialism's impersonal methods, which demand empirical proof and obscure God's presence. By embracing faith as a rational, Spirit-enabled faculty, apologists can move beyond harsh rhetoric to foster dialogue, aligning with Jesus' relational approach and inviting others to perceive God's evident presence through epistemic humility and scriptural fidelity.

16

Biblical and Theological Analysis of Tithing

TITHING, ROOTED IN THE Old Testament to support the Levites who lacked land inheritance and served in the temple (Num 18:21–24), was replaced under the new covenant by a system of voluntary giving for gospel ministry (e.g., 2 Cor 9:6–7). Malachi 3:8–10, often cited to justify tithing today, lacks clear New Testament support and is contextually tied to the Mosaic covenant. This chapter analyzes the biblical and theological basis for tithing, evaluates arguments for and against its modern practice, and clarifies New Testament teaching on giving.

BIBLICAL BACKGROUND

The Old Testament instituted tithing under the Mosaic covenant to support Levites (Num 18:21–24), fund festival celebrations, and aid the poor every three years (Deut 14:22–29; 26:12–15). Nehemiah 10:37–38 underscores tithes for temple service. Pre-Mosaic tithing appears in Abraham's voluntary tithe to Melchizedek (Gen 14:18–20) and Jacob's conditional vow (Gen 28:20–22), though not systematic. Malachi 3:8–10 accuses Israel of robbing God by withholding tithes, promising blessings for obedience within the Mosaic context.

Under the new covenant, Christ's priesthood fulfills the Levitical system, raising questions about tithing's applicability (Heb 7:11–28; 10:10–14).

ARGUMENTS FOR TITHING

Proponents argue tithing is a universal principle, citing Abraham and Jacob's pre-Mosaic examples (Gen 14:20; 28:22) as expressions of gratitude. Malachi 3:8–10 is interpreted as a moral obligation with blessings and curses applicable today.[1] Jesus' affirmation of tithing in Matt 23:23 and Luke 11:42, though critiquing Pharisaic hypocrisy, is seen as endorsing the practice. Tithing is also justified as a practical means to fund church ministries, drawing on stewardship principles (Prov 3:9–10; 1 Chr 29:14).

ARGUMENTS AGAINST TITHING

The New Testament's silence on tithing as a mandate supports its abrogation. Pre-Mosaic tithing (Gen 14:18–20; 28:22) is descriptive, and Heb 7:1–3 uses Abraham's tithe to illustrate Christ's superior priesthood, not to mandate tithing. The Levitical system, including tithing, was fulfilled in Christ (Heb 7:12; 8:6–13; 10:18). Epistles emphasize voluntary, cheerful giving (2 Cor 9:6–15; 1 Cor 16:1–2; Acts 20:35), not tithing. Malachi 3:8–10 applies to Israel, not the church, and its misuse ignores this context (Rom 10:4). Jesus' tithing comments in Matt 23:23 and Luke 11:42 address Jews under the Mosaic law, not a universal mandate. Giving is grace-based, not obligatory (2 Cor 8:1–9; Acts 11:29; Phil 4:15–18).

JUSTIFICATION OF TITHING DESPITE LACK OF SUPPORT

Denominations justify tithing by citing Mal 3:8–10 out of context, universalizing its principles.[2] Pre-Mosaic tithing (Gen 14:20; 28:22) is

---

1. Hill, *Malachi*, 317.
2. Blomberg, *Neither Poverty Nor Riches*, 90–94.

presented as normative, despite being voluntary. Jesus' words in Matt 23:23 and Luke 11:42 are prooftexted, ignoring their pre-cross context. Malachi's blessings are used pragmatically to encourage tithing, risking prosperity theology (Gal 3:13-14). Church tradition sometimes elevates tithing over scriptural clarity (Mark 7:8-9; Col 2:8).

NEW TESTAMENT GIVING

The New Testament promotes voluntary, cheerful giving (2 Cor 9:6-15), sacrificial generosity (2 Cor 8:1-5; Mark 12:41-44), support for ministry (1 Cor 16:1-2; Phil 4:15-18; 1 Tim 5:17-18), and proportional giving (Acts 11:29; 2 Cor 8:12).

COVENANTAL CONTINUITY

Covenantal continuity presumes Old Testament practices persist unless fulfilled or abrogated. The Sabbath has stronger New Testament evidence through Jesus' and the apostles' observance (Luke 4:16; Acts 13:14; 16:13; 17:2), absence of revocation, and ties to creation and eschatology (Mark 2:27-28; Heb 4:3-11; Isa 66:22-23). Tithing lacks commands, appears in critiques or typology, and yields to freewill offerings, indicating greater abrogation.

THEOLOGICAL IMPLICATIONS

Mandating tithing risks legalism (Gal 5:1; Rom 3:28), neglects grace (Rom 8:14), and misapplies Malachi's promises (Mal 3:8-10; Luke 6:35). Voluntary tithing can align with stewardship if not legalistic (1 Chr 29:14; 1 Pet 4:10).

CONCLUSION

Tithing in the Old and New Covenants

Tithing lacks New Testament support as a mandated practice, fulfilled in Christ's priesthood (Heb 7:12). The New Testament emphasizes voluntary, cheerful, and sacrificial giving (2 Cor 9:6-15; Phil 4:18).

Justifications for tithing often misapply old-covenant texts (Mal 3:8–10; Gen 14:20; 28:22; Matt 23:23). While there is no law against tithing as an act of worship, institutional mandates risk conflating loyalty with biblical giving.

A Framework for Covenantal Giving

Tithing provides a conceptual framework for how believers ought to think about giving. Giving under the old covenant was an extension of relational fidelity. Israel's very existence depended on their reciprocal relationship with God as stewards. Whenever their relationship faltered, their stewardship likewise faltered, as seen in Mal 3:8–10, where withholding tithes reflected covenantal unfaithfulness. Tithing serves to remind us that despite being in a modern economic age, we are no less dependent and are to be no less reliable in the support of God's purposes. Under the old covenant, the support directly impacted the priesthood, who represented the people to God (Num 18:21–24). Under the new covenant, giving impacts the ability of the *ekklesia* to share the gospel throughout the world, not only through denominations or Christian institutions but through the various means that God has ordained, as Paul illustrates in 1 Cor 9:7–14, where he defends support for gospel ministry. As a paradigm, tithing is not intended as a means of exploitation. Its intent is not to induce guilt for the purpose of institutional perpetuation; its purpose is to prevent exploitation by providing guidelines for covenantal reciprocity, precisely what the apostle Paul describes in 1 Cor 9, where he focuses on the spirit and attitude of giving. He also affirms charitable support of the ministry, echoing Deut 25:4, when he counsels in 1 Tim 5:18, "You shall not muzzle the ox while it is threshing," and "The laborer is worthy of his wages." Craig L. Blomberg emphasizes that New Testament giving, while voluntary, upholds the Old Testament principle of stewardship, ensuring resources support God's mission without legalistic compulsion.[3] Gordon D. Fee underscores Paul's focus in 1 Cor 9 on the heart of giving, reflecting covenantal fidelity rather than obligation.[4] Anthony C. Thiselton highlights that Paul's use of Deut 25:4 in 1 Tim 5:18 connects old-covenant

---

3. Blomberg, *1 Corinthians*, 186–88.
4. Fee, *First Epistle*, 408–10.

stewardship to new-covenant generosity, rooted in relational trust.[5] Craig S. Keener notes that Paul's emphasis on cheerful giving (2 Cor 9:7) mirrors the covenantal reciprocity of the Old Testament, fostering a community committed to God's purposes.[6]

Theological Synthesis and Implications

The chapter's analysis reveals that tithing, while not mandated under the new covenant, remains a valuable paradigm when understood as an expression of covenantal fidelity rather than a legalistic requirement. Biblical texts like 2 Cor 9:6–7 and Phil 4:15–18 emphasize giving as an act of grace, reflecting the believer's dependence on God and commitment to his mission. Theologically, tithing under the old covenant supported the priesthood's mediation, while new-covenant giving empowers the *ekklesia*'s global witness, as seen in Paul's call for generosity (1 Cor 9:7–14; Phil 4:15–18). This continuity underscores stewardship as a response to God's grace, avoiding exploitation and fostering a community of faith-driven generosity. Practically, churches should encourage giving as an act of worship and partnership in the gospel, using tithing as a guideline rather than a mandate, ensuring it reflects the cheerful, sacrificial spirit Paul advocates.

---

5. Thiselton, *First Epistle*, 660–62.
6. Keener, *1–2 Corinthians*, 78–80.

17

A Biblical Theology Undercutting Assumptions about the "Former and Latter Rain" in Joel and Acts

THE CLAIM BY SOME denominations that the "latter rain" (Joel 2:23) refers to a future outpouring of the Holy Spirit to "finish the work,"[1] in addition to its first-century fulfillment in Acts 2, lacks clear New Testament support and misinterprets the biblical context of the "former and latter rain." This chapter provides a biblical and theological critique of this view, clarifying the meaning of the "former and latter rain" and Peter's application of Joel's prophecy in Acts 2, with supporting scriptures, theological reasoning, and references.

THE MEANING OF "FORMER AND LATTER RAIN" IN CONTEXT

The phrase "former and latter rain" originates in the agricultural context of ancient Israel, where the "former rain" (*yoreh*, early rain in autumn) and "latter rain" (*malqosh*, spring rain) were essential for crop growth (Deut 11:14; Jer 5:24; cf. Zech 10:1, where God gives showers

---

1. White, *Early Writings*, 85–86.

for harvest). These rains symbolized God's provision and blessing, often tied to covenant faithfulness (Hos 6:3; Joel 2:23).[2] In Joel 2:23, the text reads:

> Be glad, O children of Zion, and rejoice in the Lord your God, for he has given the early rain for your vindication; he has poured down for you abundant rain, the early and the latter rain, as before. (ESV)

The context of Joel 2 is a call to repentance after a locust plague (Joel 1:4–20), with promises of restoration (Joel 2:18–27) and a future outpouring of God's Spirit (Joel 2:28–32). The "former and latter rain" here is part of God's promise to restore agricultural abundance, symbolizing his renewed blessing on Israel. The phrase is not inherently eschatological but reflects God's covenant faithfulness.[3] The New Testament does not use the phrase "former and latter rain" in this way. Joel 2:23 is not quoted in Acts 2, and the New Testament focuses on the singular event of the Spirit's outpouring at Pentecost as the fulfillment of Joel's prophecy (Acts 2:16–21).[4]

PETER'S USE OF JOEL 2 IN ACTS 2

In Acts 2:16–21, Peter declares that the events of Pentecost—marked by the Spirit's outpouring, tongues, and bold preaching—are the fulfillment of Joel 2:28–32:

> This is what was spoken by the prophet Joel: "And in the last days it shall be, God declares, that I will pour out my Spirit on all flesh." (Acts 2:16–17 ESV)

Peter's citation of Joel 2 emphasizes several key points:

- Fulfillment in the last days: Peter interprets Joel's prophecy as fulfilled in the events of Pentecost, signaling the arrival of the "last days" inaugurated by Christ's death, resurrection, and ascension (Acts 2:33; Heb 1:2; cf. 1 Pet 1:20, where Christ's work marks the

---

2. Stuart, *Hosea–Jonah*, 259.
3. Watts, *Joel*, 36.
4. Bruce, *Book of the Acts*, 55.

A BIBLICAL THEOLOGY UNDERCUTTING ASSUMPTIONS

last times). The "last days" encompass the entire church age, not a future eschatological period.[5]

- Universal scope: Joel's prophecy of the Spirit's outpouring "on all flesh" (Joel 2:28) is fulfilled as the Spirit is given to Jews, gentiles, men, women, young, and old (Acts 2:17–18; 10:44–45; cf. Gal 3:14, where the Spirit is the blessing for all nations). This universal scope undermines claims that a future outpouring is needed to "finish the work," as the Spirit's work is already global and ongoing (John 16:8–11).

- Connection to Christ's work: Acts 2:33 links the Spirit's outpouring to Jesus' exaltation:

  "Being therefore exalted at the right hand of God, and having received from the Father the promise of the Holy Spirit, he has poured out this that you yourselves are seeing and hearing." (ESV)

- The Pentecost event is tied to Christ's finished work, not a future event.[6]

Peter's application of Joel 2:28–32 in Acts 2:16–21 presents it as a one-time fulfillment, not a partial or preliminary event awaiting a future counterpart. The cosmic signs mentioned in Joel 2:30–31 (e.g., "blood and fire and columns of smoke" [v. 30]) are apocalyptic imagery, fulfilled symbolically in the redemptive events of Christ's death and resurrection or pointing to the final judgment (Acts 2:19–20; cf. Matt 24:29–31).[7]

CRITIQUE OF THE "LATTER RAIN" AS A FUTURE EVENT

The teaching that a future "latter rain" is necessary to "finish the work" lacks New Testament support and reveals several theological issues:

- No dual fulfillment in Acts 2: Peter's declaration, "This is what was spoken by the prophet Joel" (Acts 2:16), indicates a definitive

---

5. Longenecker, *Acts*, 272.
6. Bock, *Acts*, 110.
7. Beale, *Book of Revelation*, 44.

fulfillment, not a partial one. The New Testament does not suggest a second outpouring tied to Joel 2. Other passages about the Spirit's work (e.g., John 14:16–17; Acts 1:8; cf. John 15:26) emphasize its ongoing presence in the church, not a future escalation.[8]

- Misuse of "former and latter rain": The phrase "former and latter rain" in Joel 2:23 refers to agricultural restoration, not a spiritual outpouring. Its application to a future eschatological event is an eisegetical imposition, reading modern assumptions into the text. The New Testament never uses this phrase to describe the Spirit's work, and its use in this context distorts Joel's intent.[9]

- Theological implications: Claiming a future "latter rain" implies that the Spirit's work at Pentecost was insufficient, undermining the sufficiency of Christ's redemptive work and the Spirit's ongoing ministry (John 16:13–14; Eph 1:13–14; cf. Heb 10:12–14, where Christ's work is complete). The Great Commission (Matt 28:19–20) is empowered by the Spirit given at Pentecost, with no indication of a future outpouring needed to complete it.[10]

- Eschatological misreading: Some denominations tie the "latter rain" to end-time revival, often based on speculative interpretations of Revelation or Old Testament imagery. However, the New Testament focuses on the church's mission in the present age (Acts 1:8; 2 Tim 4:2; cf. Rev 14:6–7, where the gospel is proclaimed universally). Eschatological passages (e.g., Rev 7:9–10) depict a completed work through the redemptive events, not a second outpouring.[11]

BIBLICAL PRINCIPLES FOR CORRECT INTERPRETATION

To avoid misinterpreting Joel 2 and the "former and latter rain," biblical interpretation should follow these principles:

---

8. Bruce, *Book of the Acts*, 60.
9. Stuart, *Hosea–Jonah*, 258.
10. Keener, *Acts*, 814.
11. Beale, *Book of Revelation*, 426.

- Contextual exegesis: Interpret Joel 2:23 and 2:28–32 in their historical and literary context, recognizing the agricultural imagery of the "rains" and the eschatological fulfillment of the Spirit's outpouring in Acts 2.[12]
- New Testament priority: Let the New Testament's interpretation of Old Testament prophecy guide understanding (e.g., Peter's use of Joel in Acts 2). The apostles' inspired application is authoritative (2 Pet 1:20–21; cf. 2 Tim 3:16–17, where Scripture is God-breathed for teaching).
- Canonical unity: Ensure interpretations align with the broader biblical narrative, particularly the sufficiency of Christ's work and the Spirit's ongoing role (Heb 10:12–14; John 14:26; cf. 1 Cor 12:13, where the Spirit unites the *ekklesia*).
- Avoid speculation: Reject interpretations that rely on extra-biblical assumptions or metaphors (e.g., finishing the work) not grounded in Scripture.[13]

CONCLUSION

The teaching of a future "latter rain" tied to Joel 2 misinterprets the biblical text and Peter's application in Acts 2. The "former and latter rain" in Joel 2:23 refers to agricultural blessing, not a dual outpouring of the Spirit. Peter presents Pentecost as the fulfillment of Joel 2:28–32, linked to Christ's finished work (Acts 2:33), with no New Testament evidence for a future outpouring to "finish the work." This view risks undermining the sufficiency of the Spirit's current empowerment and the unity of God's redemptive plan. Proper exegesis, rooted in context and New Testament authority, clarifies that the Spirit's outpouring at Pentecost equips the *ekklesia* for its mission until Christ's return.

---

12. Fee and Stuart, *How to Read*, 203.
13. Wright, *New Testament*, 140.

18

The Permanence of the Clean/Unclean Distinction

A Covenantal and Moral Framework for Understanding Covenantal Violations as Spiritual Rebellion

THE CLEAN/UNCLEAN DISTINCTION (*TAHOR/SHEQETS/TAME*) in the Mosaic law, as articulated in Lev 11 and Deut 14, is frequently interpreted as a temporary ritual regulation specific to Israel's theocratic covenant, purportedly fulfilled in the New Covenant (e.g., Mark 7:19; Acts 10:15). This chapter contends that the distinction is a permanent, creation-based standard, rooted in God's holiness (Gen 7:2–3; Lev 11:44–45; Isa 66:17). All covenantal violations, including the consumption of *sheqets* (abominable foods), constitute moral offenses as they represent spiritual rebellion against God's covenant law. By "moral permanence," this study refers to the enduring moral significance of such infractions until addressed through forgiveness (for spiritual rebellion) or cleansing (for ritual impurity). This position challenges New Testament interpretations influenced by a priori assumptions of impermanence, which misrepresent the continuity of God's holiness across covenants. The distinction, exemplified by the seven pairs of clean animals (*tehorah*) versus two pairs of unclean animals (*asher lo tehorah*) in Gen 7:2–3, reflects God's eternal design. Violations are not minor infractions but assaults on the

THE PERMANENCE OF THE CLEAN/UNCLEAN DISTINCTION

covenant and God's holiness, requiring redress. This chapter articulates this thesis through biblical texts, Jewish theological perspectives, and a critique of New Testament interpretations, with a particular focus on the permanence of the "fit" versus "unfit" designation for animals in food and sacrifice.

THE CLEAN/UNCLEAN DISTINCTION AS A PERMANENT, CREATION-BASED STANDARD

The clean/unclean distinction originates in Gen 7:2–3, where God instructs Noah to take seven pairs of clean animals (*behemah hatehorah*) and two pairs of unclean animals (*asher lo tehorah*) onto the ark.[1] The terms *tehorah* (from *tahor*, meaning "clean" or "pure") and its negation (*lo tehorah*, "not clean") predate the Mosaic law, indicating a creation-based standard embedded in God's design.[2] The larger number of clean animals likely served practical purposes (e.g., sacrifice, Gen 8:20; sustenance, Gen 9:3) and theological ones, reflecting God's holiness and covenantal order.[3] The term *tehorah* denotes animals suitable for God's purposes, including consumption and sacrifice, aligning with divine purity, while unclean animals (*tame* or *sheqets*) were unfit, possibly due to symbolic impurity or ecological roles.[4]

This distinction is codified in Lev 11 and Deut 14, which explicitly link *tahor* to animals permissible for consumption and *tame/sheqets* to those forbidden. Leviticus 11:46–47 summarizes: "This is the law regarding the animal . . . to make a distinction between the unclean and the clean, and between the edible creature and the creature which is not to be eaten." This parallel construction equates *tahor* with "edible" and *tame* (or *lo tehorah*) with "not to be eaten," establishing that cleanliness denotes edibility and uncleanness denotes unsuitability for food (Lev 11:3–8, 13–19, 43, 46–47; Deut 14:4–6, 11–12, 19–20; Lev 20:25–26). The purpose is tied to Israel's call to holiness: "For I am the Lord your God. Consecrate yourselves therefore, and be holy, because I am holy" (Lev 11:44–45; cf. Lev 20:25–26, which separates Israel as God's people).

---

1. Wenham, *Genesis 1–15*, 177.
2. Wenham, *Genesis 1–15*, 177.
3. Walton, *Genesis*, 310.
4. Milgrom, *Leviticus*, 691.

The Sifra on Lev 11:47 reinforces this by emphasizing discernment between clean and unclean species, affirming *tehorah* as fit for food within the framework of divine purity.⁵

The permanence of this standard is further evidenced in Isa 66:17, which condemns eating *sheqets* foods (e.g., swine, mice) in an eschatological context of idolatrous rebellion, suggesting enduring moral significance.⁶ Jewish theologians, such as Maimonides and David H. Stern, argue that dietary laws remain eternal for Jews, rooted in God's covenant and holiness.⁷

MORAL PERMANENCE OF COVENANTAL VIOLATIONS

All violations of the Mosaic covenant, including pre-Mosaic ones like consuming *sheqets* foods, are moral offenses because they defy God's covenant law, constituting spiritual rebellion. In the theocracy, sin is defined by the law (Deut 4:5–8; Rom 7:7; cf. 1 John 3:4), and no one is saved outside the covenant. Thus, infractions—whether idolatry (*to'ebah*, Deut 7:25) or eating *sheqets* (Lev 11:7)—are assaults on God's holiness, requiring forgiveness or cleansing to resolve their moral permanence. Willful disobedience reflects spiritual rebellion, necessitating forgiveness (Num 15:30–31; Lev 16:30), while eating *sheqets* renders one ritually impure (*tame*, Lev 11:43), requiring cleansing.⁸ Isaiah 66:17 illustrates this, condemning "those who sanctify and purify themselves ... Who eat pig's flesh, detestable things [*sheqets*], and mice," where eating *sheqets* is part of idolatrous rebellion, carrying moral weight.⁹

UNFITNESS FOR CONSUMPTION AND THE LIKELIHOOD OF TEMPORALITY VERSUS PERMANENCE

The designation of animals as "fit" (*tahor/tehorah*) or "unfit" (*tame/sheqets*) for consumption and sacrifice is central to the covenant's

---

5. Finkelstein, *Sifra on Leviticus*, Shemini, Parashat 11, 2:201.

6. Oswalt, *Book of Isaiah*, 672.

7. Maimonides, *Mishneh Torah, Hilchot Ma'akhalot Asurot*, 1:1–2; Stern, *Restoring the Jewishness*, 45.

8. Klawans, *Impurity and Sin*, 32.

9. Oswalt, *Book of Isaiah*, 672.

THE PERMANENCE OF THE CLEAN/UNCLEAN DISTINCTION

reflection of God's holiness (Lev 11:44–45; Deut 14:2, 21). Leviticus 11 and Deut 14 explicitly tie *tahor* to animals suitable for food and sacrifice, while *tame* or *sheqets* denotes those unfit: "You may eat any clean bird. But these are the ones that you shall not eat: the eagle and the vulture and the buzzard" (Deut 14:11–12; cf. Lev 11:13–19).

This distinction, rooted in creation (Gen 7:2–3), underscores that *tehorah* animals align with God's purposes, while unfit animals defile Israel's holiness if consumed (Lev 11:43; Lev 20:25–26). Violations, even if construed as ritual, impinge on God's holiness, carrying moral weight due to their defiance of the covenant.[10]

The question of whether animals deemed unfit (*lo tehorah* or *tame*) could later become fit challenges the permanence of this standard. Some interpreters cite Mark 7:19 to suggest a miraculous change, implying that Jesus altered the Mosaic covenant before its fulfillment at the cross. However, the Greek text (*katharizōn panta ta brōmata*, "purifying all foods") and context (Mark 7:18–20) focus on defilement from the heart, not dietary laws. Jesus addresses Pharisaic handwashing traditions, affirming that permitted foods (*tahor*) do not defile if eaten with unwashed hands, as they pass through the stomach and are eliminated (Mark 7:19). To assert that Jesus declared *sheqets* foods fit dismisses the cultural and covenantal context, lacking textual support for such a change.

CLEAN/UNCLEAN SIGNIFICANCE AND GOD'S HOLINESS

The clean/unclean distinction's significance lies in maintaining Israel's covenantal holiness, enabling God's presence in the theocracy (Lev 15:31; Ezek 44:23). Clean animals (*tahor*) were suitable for sacrifice (Lev 1:2–3) and consumption (Deut 14:4–6), symbolizing Israel's set-apart status (Exod 19:6). Unclean animals (*sheqets/tame*) defiled this status if consumed (Lev 11:43). Leviticus 20:25–26 emphasizes this separation:

> "You are therefore to make a distinction between the clean animal and the unclean. . . . So you are to be holy to Me, for I the Lord am holy; and I have singled you out from the peoples to be Mine."

---

10. Klawans, *Impurity and Sin*, 36.

Violations disrupted God's presence, requiring cleansing (Lev 11:24–28) or atonement for intentional acts (Lev 7:20). In the theocracy, all laws—moral, ritual, civil—were unified under God's holiness, making disobedience spiritual rebellion (Deut 4:5–8).

CRITIQUE OF POPULAR NEW TESTAMENT INTERPRETATIONS

Popular interpretations of Mark 7:19, as well as Acts 10:15 ("What God has cleansed, no longer consider unholy") and Rom 14:14 ("I know and am convinced in the Lord Jesus that nothing is unclean in itself"), often assume the clean/unclean distinction is impermanent, fulfilled in Christ (Heb 10:1–14). These readings, influenced by supersessionist assumptions, overlook the covenantal context and continuity of God's holiness (1 Pet 1:15–16; Heb 12:14). In Mark 7:19, Jesus critiques external defilement, not dietary laws. The translation that results in Mark's parenthetical interpretation "he declared all foods clean" appears to be in tension with a plain reading of the Greek text and the general context of the first century. More accurately, "[it] passed into the belly and goes out into the sewer, purifying all foods."

Acts 10:15 concerns gentile inclusion (cf. Acts 10:28), not a nullification of *sheqets* distinctions, as Acts 15:20 retains restrictions for gentiles (e.g., blood).[11] Romans 14:14 and 1 Tim 4:4–5 address food offered to idols, not *sheqets* foods, reflecting gentile freedom, not abrogation of Jewish covenantal standards.[12]

ENGAGEMENT WITH COUNTERARGUMENTS

Opponents argue that the clean/unclean distinction is covenant-specific, citing the allowance in Deut 14:21 for foreigners to eat *nebelah* (a clean animal that dies of itself) and New Testament texts nullifying dietary laws (Mark 7:19; Acts 10:15). They distinguish ritual violations (*sheqets*, reversible through cleansing, Lev 11:24–28) from moral violations (*to'ebah*, 1 Cor 10:14), viewing *sheqets* as fulfilled in Christ (Col

---

11. Bock, *Acts*, 503.
12. Schreiner, *Law and Its Fulfillment*, 254.

2:16–17).[13] However, Deut 14:21 underscores Israel's unique role, not a universal abrogation. New Testament texts address specific contexts (gentile inclusion, idol-related food), not *sheqets* distinctions.[14] The moral permanence of *sheqets* violations lies in their defiance of God's holiness, requiring forgiveness or cleansing.[15] The theocracy's holistic law equates all disobedience with spiritual rebellion (Num 15:30–31; Deut 6:25).

CONCLUSION

The clean/unclean distinction (*tahor/sheqets*) is a permanent, creation-based standard rooted in God's holiness (Gen 7:2–3; Lev 11:44–45; Isa 66:17). The designation of animals as fit (*tehorah*) or unfit (*tame/sheqets*) for consumption and sacrifice reflects divine purposes, and no textual evidence supports a change from unfit to fit, as misinterpretations of Mark 7:19 suggest. All covenantal violations are moral offenses, constituting spiritual rebellion and requiring forgiveness or cleansing to resolve their moral permanence. The apostle Peter exhorts the saints to holiness (1 Pet 1:16), quoting from Lev 11:44 (dietary restriction), Lev 19:2 (a warning against idolatry), and Lev 20:7 (a warning against immorality), demonstrating the continuity of holiness between the covenants. New Testament interpretations assuming impermanence (Mark 7:19; Acts 10:15) are influenced by supersessionist assumptions, misrepresenting the continuity of God's holiness. Jewish theologians affirm the distinction's permanence and moral weight, supporting the thesis that violations are assaults on God's covenant, not minor infractions. The biblical and theological witness underscores the enduring significance of covenantal obedience, with forgiveness or cleansing as the only resolution for infractions.

---

13. Milgrom, *Leviticus*, 686.
14. Mark 7:19; Acts 10:15; Rom 14:14; 1 Tim 4:4–5.
15. Maimonides, *Mishneh Torah, Hilkhot Teshuvah*, 1:1–4; Klawans, *Impurity and Sin*, 36.

19

Kings, Queens, and the Gang That Won
A Deconstruction of Romans 13 and Divine Authority

THE TEXT OF ROM 13:1–7 has been wielded throughout history as a theological justification for political authority, particularly in the context of monarchical absolutism and totalitarian regimes. The passage, which instructs believers to submit to governing authorities as divinely ordained, has been a cornerstone for the doctrine of the divine right of kings and has been extended to legitimize various forms of authoritarian rule. This chapter deconstructs the use of Rom 13:1–7 to support monarchical and totalitarian claims to divine authority, arguing that such interpretations sanitize the violent and pragmatic origins of political power. By examining the historical and biblical context alongside scholarly critiques, this chapter reveals that rulers, often romanticized as divinely appointed, were frequently the beneficiaries of conquest, alliances, and strategic maneuvering—essentially, the "gang that won." This perspective challenges the notion of divine ordination and highlights the text's misuse to justify oppression.

EXEGETICAL CONTEXT OF ROMANS 13:1–7

Romans 13 begins with the injunction,

> Let every person be subject to the governing authorities. For there is no authority except from God, and those which exist are established by God. (Rom 13:1)

At face value, this text appears to endorse unconditional obedience to secular rulers. However, the historical and literary context suggests a more nuanced intention. Written during the reign of the Roman Empire under Nero, Paul's words were addressed to a Christian community navigating life under a pagan regime. Scholars such as John Barton and John Muddiman argue that Paul's instruction does not legitimize every exercise of civil authority or mandate absolute obedience. Instead, it reflects a pragmatic call for Christians to cooperate with authorities to avoid persecution, particularly in the wake of the expulsion of Jews (including Jewish Christians) from Rome under Emperor Claudius (AD 41–54).[1] The passage is not a blanket endorsement of all governments but a situational exhortation to maintain order within a specific sociopolitical context.

Furthermore, the text must be read alongside other biblical passages that qualify submission to authority. Acts 5:29, where Peter and the apostles declare, "We must obey God rather than men," establishes a clear limit to obedience when human authorities contradict divine law. Similarly, Dan 2:21 ("He removes kings and appoints kings"), often cited to support divine ordination, is balanced by Daniel's narrative of resistance to unjust rulers, such as Nebuchadnezzar and Darius. These texts suggest that divine sovereignty over authorities does not preclude resistance to tyranny or oppression.

THE DIVINE RIGHT OF KINGS: HISTORICAL AND THEOLOGICAL FOUNDATIONS

The doctrine of the divine right of kings, which gained prominence in Europe during the sixteenth and seventeenth centuries, asserted that monarchs derived their authority directly from God, rendering them unaccountable to earthly powers such as parliaments or the church. King James I of England, a key proponent, articulated this in his writings, stating,

---

1. Barton and Muddiman, *Oxford Bible Commentary*, 1084.

> The state of monarchy is the supremest thing upon earth: for kings are not only God's lieutenants upon earth, and sit upon God's throne, but even by God himself they are called gods.[2]

This doctrine drew heavily on Rom 13:1–7, interpreting Paul's words as a divine mandate for absolute monarchical rule.

However, this interpretation ignores the complex historical origins of monarchies. As the chapter notes, many monarchs were the "gang that won"—products of conquest, clan rivalries, strategic marriages, and alliances rather than divine selection. For example, the consolidation of power by European monarchs often involved violent clan rivalries, bribery, and intermarriage to secure dynastic control, as seen in the Habsburg and Tudor dynasties. The romanticized image of monarchs as divinely ordained was a theological veneer that sanitized their often ruthless ascent to power. Scholars like Glenn Burgess argue that divine-right theory was less about genuine religious conviction and more about quashing opposition, particularly from religious groups like Catholics and Puritans who challenged royal authority.[3]

Theological support for the divine right of kings also drew from Old Testament examples, such as God's anointing of Saul and David (1 Sam 8:1–22; 16:13). However, these texts highlight the conditional nature of divine appointment—Saul was rejected for disobedience, and David's dynasty was sustained only through fidelity to God's covenant. The selective use of Rom 13:1–7 to justify absolute monarchy overlooks these qualifications, as well as the broader biblical narrative of prophetic critique against unjust rulers (e.g., Nathan's rebuke of David in 2 Sam 12:7–12).

EXTENSION TO TOTALITARIAN REGIMES

The misuse of Rom 13:1–7 extends beyond monarchies to modern totalitarian regimes, which have invoked divine authority to justify oppressive governance. The chapter's assertion that the assumptions of divine authority have been co-opted by world governments finds support in historical examples. For instance, during the American Revolution, loyalists used Rom 13 to advocate obedience to the British crown,

---

2. James I, *True Law*, 53–70.
3. Burgess, *Politics of the Ancient*, 45–47.

while anti-abolitionists in the nineteenth century cited it to defend slavery, arguing that submission to authority included compliance with unjust laws like the Fugitive Slave Act of 1850.[4] Similarly, in the twentieth century, some German churches appealed to Rom 13 to justify compliance with Nazi policies, though others, like Dietrich Bonhoeffer, resisted such interpretations, emphasizing obedience to God over human authorities.[5]

Theologians like Ernst Käsemann and Paul Tillich have critiqued the use of Rom 13 to support authoritarianism. Käsemann argues that the passage reflects a "hermeneutic of conscience," where submission is conditional on the ruler's alignment with God's justice.[6] Tillich warns against interpretations that cast Rom 13 as an anti-revolutionary mandate, noting that such readings have been used to suppress legitimate resistance to tyranny.[7] These critiques align with the chapter's argument that divine authority has been manipulated to legitimize regimes that are, in reality, the products of power struggles rather than divine will.

RESPONSES TO THEOLOGICAL AND HISTORICAL CHALLENGES

A primary objection to this deconstruction is that Rom 13:1–7 explicitly commands submission to all governing authorities, implying divine endorsement of their rule. However, scholars like N. T. Wright counter that Paul's intent was not to legitimize every government but to affirm God's sovereignty over human authorities, who are accountable to divine justice.[8] This is supported by John Calvin's view that obedience is conditional on the ruler's adherence to God's law, and resistance is justified when authorities act unjustly.[9]

Another challenge is the historical reliance on divine-right theology by Christian monarchs and churches. While figures like James I and Louis XIV invoked Rom 13 to consolidate power, this chapter argues

---

4. Davis, *Problem of Slavery*, 83–85.
5. Bonhoeffer, *Ethics*, 346–47.
6. Käsemann, *Commentary on Romans*, 352–53.
7. Tillich, *Systematic Theology*, 384–85.
8. Wright, *Paul and the Faithfulness*, 1306–8.
9. Calvin, *Institutes*, 4.20.31–32.

that their authority often stemmed from pragmatic and violent means rather than divine mandate. The French Revolution and the American Declaration of Independence, which rejected divine-right claims in favor of popular sovereignty, further undermine the doctrine's legitimacy.[10] Thomas Jefferson's assertion that "all men are created equal" directly challenges the hierarchical assumptions of divine-right theory,[11] aligning with biblical principles of justice and human dignity (Gal 3:28).

Finally, the chapter's characterization of monarchs as the "gang that won" may be criticized as overly reductive. However, historical analyses, such as those by Katy Schiel, demonstrate that monarchies often emerged from clan rivalries and strategic alliances, with divine-right rhetoric serving as a post hoc justification.[12] This perspective is reinforced by the Catholic doctrine of tyrannicide, which permitted resistance to unjust rulers, indicating that even within divine-right frameworks, authority was not absolute.[13]

BROADER IMPLICATIONS AND THEOLOGICAL RECONSTRUCTION

The deconstruction of Rom 13:1–7 as a tool for monarchical and totalitarian legitimacy has profound implications for Christian political theology. By exposing the pragmatic and often violent origins of political authority, the chapter challenges believers to critically evaluate claims of divine ordination. The biblical narrative consistently portrays God as siding with the oppressed against unjust rulers (e.g., Exod 3:7–10; Amos 5:24), suggesting that divine authority is not a blank check for tyranny but a call to justice.

This perspective aligns with modern liberation theologies, which emphasize God's preferential option for the marginalized. Gustavo Gutiérrez argues that biblical texts like Rom 13 must be interpreted in light of God's justice, not as endorsements of oppressive structures.[14]

---

10. Wood, *Creation*, 91–93.
11. Jefferson, *Declaration of Independence*, 429.
12. Schiel, *Monarchy*, 22–24.
13. Bainton, *Reformation*, 147–49.
14. Gutiérrez, *Theology of Liberation*, 155–57.

Similarly, the chapter's critique of sanitized monarchies resonates with these theological frameworks.

CONCLUSION

Romans 13:1–7 has been historically misused to justify monarchical absolutism and totalitarian regimes, portraying rulers as divinely ordained. However, a closer examination reveals that Paul's instruction was contextually specific and does not endorse unconditional obedience. The divine right of kings, and its extension to modern authoritarianism, often served as a theological veneer for the "gang that won"—rulers who consolidated power through conquest and manipulation. By deconstructing this narrative, this chapter invites Christians to prioritize God's justice over blind submission, fostering a theology that champions human dignity and resists oppression.

20

Institutional Authority and the Queer Identified

SOCIAL CONTROVERSIES ARE NOTHING new to the church. They are as old as cultural clashes. What is new is the LGBTQIA (queer) issue. Some may argue that it is addressed in the Bible in principle, while others will argue that there simply is no cultural equivalent because it's a different time and place. The intent of this chapter is not to argue one way or the other but simply to provide support for the idea that it doesn't really matter one way or the other.

Churches make rules, policies, and decisions based on an assumption of divine authority to make and/or enforce such rules, but what if they do not really have the authority? What if their authority is purely attributional and supported only by consensus? What if a person's standing before God is determined by Christ alone, who said,

> My sheep listen to My voice, and I know them, and they follow Me; and I give them eternal life, and they will never perish; and no one will snatch them out of My hand. My Father, who has given them to Me, is greater than all; and no one is able to snatch them out of the Father's hand. I and the Father are one. (John 10:27–30)

Could it be that churches have inserted themselves as the keepers of the gate, assuming that "the church" is synonymous with the *ekklesia*?

INSTITUTIONAL AUTHORITY AND THE QUEER IDENTIFIED

Is it possible that they have equated their voices with the voice of the Shepherd and expect to be followed?

I am proposing that institutional organizations are not the *ekklesia* or the proxy for her. They are hierarchical structures that presume to exercise her prerogatives in determining who can and cannot pass through the gate. They are propped up on two crutches, history and tradition, neither of which provide a sufficient foundation for divine authority. By substituting the word *ekklesia* for the word "church," they have—in many ways—usurped the role of the Spirit of God and erected barriers, making it difficult for struggling people to get to God.

> But woe to you, scribes and Pharisees, hypocrites, because you shut the kingdom of heaven in front of people; for you do not enter it yourselves, nor do you allow those who are entering to go in. (Matt 23:13)

The confusion is resolved when we understand not only what Jesus said but what he meant in Matt 13:24–30:

> Jesus presented another parable to them, saying, "The kingdom of heaven is like a man who sowed good seed in his field. But while his men were sleeping, his enemy came and sowed weeds among the wheat, and left. And when the wheat sprouted and produced grain, then the weeds also became evident. And the slaves of the landowner came and said to him, 'Sir, did you not sow good seed in your field? How then does it have weeds?' And he said to them, 'An enemy has done this!' The slaves said to him, 'Do you want us, then, to go and gather them up?' But he said, 'No; while you are gathering up the weeds, you may uproot the wheat with them. Allow both to grow together until the harvest; and at the time of the harvest I will say to the reapers, "First gather up the weeds and bind them in bundles to burn them; but gather the wheat into my barn."'

Clearly, the point is that the wheat and the tares may be connected at the root and/or entangled; so, both are to be allowed to "grow together until the harvest." It's highly unlikely that this strategy could be successfully employed in a "church"; it is far more likely to succeed in the *ekklesia*, where Jesus is able to discern—despite entangled roots—who is his. Additionally, our limited knowledge of a person's spiritual journey cripples our ability to make judgments that only God can make. The organization is frequently fooled by the appearance of things and not infrequently errs in granting privilege to those with social status, whereas the intimate knowledge where speech and audial reception intersect—"My sheep hear My voice, and I know them"—is the domain of Christ alone.

This is true not only for queer-identifying individuals but for anyone claiming Jesus as Lord and Savior; it is Jesus who gets to make that determination based on information that has not been revealed to us. Why? Because our anemic understanding of sin precludes the necessary knowledge to make judgments about such matters. Our "expertise" in the externals is reductionistic, and with respect to matters of the heart, our best guess is that good people do what is good and bad people do what is bad, and we tend toward blindness when it comes to those progressions through which the Spirit of God works in the life of an individual.

We've looked past those lucid reminders stating,

> Therefore you have no excuse, you foolish person, everyone of you who passes judgment; for in that matter in which you judge someone else, you condemn yourself; for you who judge practice the same things. And we know that the judgment of God rightly falls upon those who practice such things. But do you suppose this, you foolish person who passes judgment on those who practice such things, and yet does them as well, that you will escape the judgment of God? Or do you think lightly of the riches of His kindness and restraint and patience, not knowing that the kindness of God leads you to repentance? (Rom 2:1–4)

The present active indicative verb ἄγει insists that he is leading, i.e., leading the individual to repentance. And it shouldn't need to be said, but on his timetable and not yours.

THE INSTITUTIONAL CHURCH AS GATEKEEPER: ATTRIBUTION AND CONSENSUS VS. DIVINE AUTHORITY

The institutional church often assumes a role as gatekeeper, determining who is worthy of inclusion based on human-constructed rules, policies, and doctrines. This assumption of authority is attributional—derived from self-assigned titles and historical claims—and supported by consensus among its members and leaders. As explored in chapter 11,

INSTITUTIONAL AUTHORITY AND THE QUEER IDENTIFIED

the institutional church's hierarchy and creeds create barriers that the *ekklesia*, as an organic body, does not require (Matt 23:13). For queer individuals, this gatekeeping manifests in debates over membership, marriage, and ministry, where institutions that presume to speak for Christ speak in a multitude of tongues with many voices; and it is their institutional right.

Yet, Scripture affirms that true authority rests with Christ alone, who knows his sheep intimately and grants eternal life without human mediation (John 10:27-30). The institutional church's voice is not the Shepherd's voice nor the voice of a surrogate; it is a human echo, often distorted by power dynamics and cultural biases. By equating itself with the *ekklesia*, the institution usurps the Spirit's role, often erecting barriers that prevent struggling individuals from accessing God's grace. This substitution not only confuses attribution and consensus with divine ordination but also risks condemning those whom Christ may be leading through unpredictable means to repentance (Rom 2:4).

Theologians like Karl Barth have critiqued this institutional overreach, arguing that the church's authority is derived and conditional, serving as a witness to Christ rather than a substitute for him.[1] Similarly, Dietrich Bonhoeffer warned against "cheap grace" that institutions dispense through rules, emphasizing that true discipleship involves costly obedience to Christ, not fealty to human structures.[2] For queer individuals, this means their spiritual journey is discerned by Christ, not by consensus-driven policies that may reflect cultural prejudice rather than divine will.

THE WHEAT AND TARES PARABLE: ENTANGLED ROOTS AND DIVINE DISCERNMENT

Jesus' parable of the wheat and tares (Matt 13:24-30) provides a profound metaphor for understanding why institutions cannot reliably judge spiritual standing, particularly in complex issues like queer identity. The enemy sows tares among the wheat while the landowner's servants sleep, and the two grow together, often entangled at the root. The servants' zeal to uproot the tares risks destroying the wheat, prompting

---

1. Barth, *Church Dogmatics*, 4/3.1, 688-90.
2. Bonhoeffer, *Cost of Discipleship*, 45-60.

the landowner to command, "Allow both to grow together until the harvest" (Matt 13:30).

This parable underscores the danger of premature judgment: human gatekeepers, limited by external appearances, cannot see the entangled roots of sin and grace in a person's life. Institutions, with their policies and creeds, often attempt to "weed out" those deemed unworthy, but this risks uprooting genuine faith. In the *ekklesia*, discernment belongs to Christ, who knows the heart and separates wheat from tares at the harvest (Matt 13:41–43). Unimpeded by history and tradition, he reads people's hearts in real time and is never stingy toward them with grace. For queer individuals claiming Christ as Lord, their "entangled roots"—the interplay of identity, sin, and grace—may be invisible to human eyes but are fully known to the Shepherd.

N. T. Wright interprets this parable as a warning against self-righteous judgment, emphasizing God's patience in allowing growth until the end.[3] Similarly, Augustine's concept of the *corpus permixtum* (mixed body) recognizes that true and false believers coexist in the visible church, with separation reserved for God.[4] Institutions that exclude based on identity risk violating this principle, assuming a role reserved for Christ.

ANEMIC UNDERSTANDING OF SIN: THE LIMITS OF INSTITUTIONAL JUDGMENT

Institutions often judge queer individuals based on an *anemic understanding of sin*, reducing it to external behaviors while ignoring the heart's complexities (Jer 17:9). This reductionism fails to account for the Spirit's work in leading individuals to repentance through kindness (Rom 2:4). Paul's warning in Rom 2:1–4 condemns those who judge others while practicing similar sins, reminding us that God's patience—his leading (*agei*) to repentance—is personal and timed by him, not institutions.

For queer individuals, this means their spiritual journey cannot be fully assessed by external standards; only Christ, who knows the entangled roots of sin and grace, can judge rightly. Institutions, fooled by

---

3. Wright, *Matthew for Everyone*, 171–74.
4. Augustine, *City of God*, trans. Bettenson, 20.9 (828–30).

appearances, err in privileging social status or conformity, as seen in the critique of partiality in Jas 2:1-4. Theologians like James Cone critique institutional blindness to systemic sin, arguing that true discernment emerges from the marginalized, where the Spirit reveals God's justice.[5] An anemic view of sin leads to blindness in judging queer lives, ignoring the progressions through which the Spirit transforms hearts and lives.

THEOLOGICAL CHALLENGES: USURPING THE SPIRIT AND ERECTING BARRIERS

By presuming to be the gatekeepers, institutions usurp the Spirit's role in guiding believers into truth (John 16:13). This results in barriers for queer individuals that often shut off the kingdom as the scribes and Pharisees did (Matt 23:13). The *ekklesia*, as an organism, operates on organic unity, where membership is determined by Christ's call and the response of individuals to it, not human creeds (John 10:27). Institutions, with their attributional authority, equate consensus that sustains them with divine will, but this is a distortion, as Barth warns: the church's authority is witness to, not substitute for, God's Word.[6]

For queer believers, this means their inclusion is not subject to institutional vote but to Christ's discernment. The *ekklesia*'s oneness (Gal 3:28) focuses on faithfulness to the Shepherd.

CONCLUSION

To be clear, I'm not arguing for/against queer inclusion but simply focusing on the lack of institutional authority on the basis of the Bible. Jesus has not delegated judgment in such matters to any church institution. In the Scriptures, Jesus emphasizes entangled roots, Christ's discernment and authority, and God's leading to repentance.

The queer issue highlights the tension between institutional gatekeeping and the *ekklesia*'s organic unity under Christ. Institutions, with attributional authority, erect barriers based on consensus, but true standing is determined by the Shepherd who knows his sheep (John 10:27-30). The wheat and tares parable warns against premature

---

5. Cone, *Cross*, 150-65.
6. Barth, *Church Dogmatics*, 4/1, 688-90.

judgment, as entangled roots defy human discernment (Matt 13:24–30). Our limited knowledge of a person's spiritual journey cripples our ability to make judgments that only God can make. By contrast, God's kindness leads to repentance (Rom 2:1–4). The *ekklesia*, unbound by human pretexts, welcomes all who know and trust the voice of Christ, and he knows them.

Postscript
Theology as Art and Science—The Divine Invitation to Progressive Revelation

THEOLOGY, AT ITS ESSENCE, is both art and science—a divinely ordained craft that marries the precision of inquiry with the creativity of interpretation. As science, it demands rigorous scrutiny, contextual exegesis, and a willingness to measure assumptions against the full counsel of Scripture, much like the carpenter's proverb that inspires this volume: measure twice, cut once. As art, it invites the imagination to explore the depths of divine mystery, fostering expressions of faith that transcend rigid formulas and embrace the dynamic unfolding of God's truth. This dual nature satisfies the human thirst for progressive revelation, as God has not left us with static dogmas but with a living Word that reveals himself progressively through time, circumstance, and the Spirit's illumination (Heb 1:1-2; John 16:13). In the chapters of this work, from reappraising divorce as a covenantal rupture to deconstructing the "spiritual gifts" fallacy as manifestations of the Spirit rather than personal endowments, we see theology in action: a disciplined pursuit that challenges inherited assumptions and uncovers layers of meaning intended for our moral and spiritual growth.

The virtues of theology are manifold yet too often taken for granted amid the history that has shaped our doctrines. Inquiry, humility, and fidelity to Scripture form its core, virtues exemplified in the Berean spirit of Acts 17:11, where noble believers examined the Scriptures daily to verify Paul's teachings. These qualities have propelled theological progress, from the early church councils clarifying Christ's divinity to the Reformation's recovery of justification by faith. Yet, we seldom

POSTSCRIPT

pause to appreciate how our teachings—on the Sabbath as ineradicable holiness (chapter 7), the soul as a conditional "soul-print" (chapter 9), or the *ekklesia* as an organic body distinct from institutional hierarchies (chapter 11)—emerged from generations of faithful wrestling with God's word. History reveals that doctrines are not divine dictations dropped from heaven but the fruit of communal discernment, often forged in controversy and refined through error. We inherit them as gifts, but taking them for granted risks stagnation, as if the Spirit's work ceased with our forebears.

Dogmatism, however, borders on fearful superstition when it resists this progressive spirit, transforming theology from a living dialogue into a fortified idol. Throughout history, such rigidity has led to persecution, as if God calls us to defend dogmas by the blade or the barrel rather than by reasoned faith. The Inquisition's flames, the Salem witch trials, and even modern excommunications of critical thinkers echo this pattern: fear of uncertainty masquerading as zeal for truth. As Jesus warned the scribes and Pharisees,

> "You shut the kingdom of heaven in front of people; for you do not enter it yourselves, nor do you allow those who are entering to go in." (Matt 23:13)

When dogmatism prevails, it stifles the very inquiry that God ordains for our maturation, turning theology into a weapon rather than a tool for liberation.

Jesus himself modeled this scrutiny in his critique of traditions that obscured God's intent:

> "You examine the Scriptures because you think that in them you have eternal life; and it is those very Scriptures that testify about Me; and yet you are unwilling to come to Me so that you may have life." (John 5:39–40)

Here, he exposes the folly of idolizing the text while missing its purpose—to lead us to him, the source of eternal life. Our search is for Jesus and the eternal life he offers, or at least it ought to be. With this goal in mind, we can be confident that our errors will be overcome by light, for we are not called to be right but to be faithful. Faithfulness embraces the art of theology as a humble pursuit, measuring twice not out of doubt but out of reverence, trusting that the Spirit guides us into all truth

(John 16:13). In this way, theology becomes a means of grace, drawing us closer to the God who reveals himself progressively, not to satisfy our intellect alone, but to transform our lives in covenantal obedience. May this volume inspire such faithful inquiry, reminding us that the ultimate measure is Christ himself, in whom all truth finds its fulfillment.

About the Author

JEROME C. CRICHTON, DMIN, PHD, is an interdisciplinary scholar whose research bridges theology, psychology, sociology, and cultural critique. He holds doctoral degrees in ministry and psychology from United Theological Seminary (Dayton, Ohio) and Alliant International University (San Francisco Bay Area), and his work engages covenantal ethics, epistemology, and ritual studies with intellectual rigor and cultural sensitivity. His scholarship speaks to graduate students, academics, and reflective readers navigating contested domains of meaning and justice.

Dr. Crichton serves as adjunct professor of psychology at Alliant International University and Diablo Valley Community College in the San Francisco Bay Area. He is also senior pastor at Every Word Ministries, where he integrates scholarly insight with pastoral practice. In addition to his academic work, he is a recording artist with two solo albums—*Celebratin' Good Dayze* (2014) and *TransAtlantic Journey* (2025)—which explore themes of identity, spiritual connection, and cultural reflection.

Bibliography

Achtemeier, Paul J. *Inspiration and Authority: Nature and Function of Christian Scripture.* Peabody, MA: Hendrickson, 1996.
Adams, Marilyn McCord. *Horrendous Evils and the Goodness of God.* Ithaca, NY: Cornell University Press, 1999.
Aquinas, Thomas. *Summa Theologica.* Translated by the Fathers of the English Dominican Province. New York: Benziger Bros., 1947.
Aristotle. *De Anima.* Translated by Christopher Shields. Oxford: Oxford University Press, 2016.
Athanasius. *On the Incarnation.* Translated by John Behr. Yonkers, NY: St Vladimir's Seminary Press, 2011.
Augustine. *City of God.* Translated by Henry Bettenson. Penguin Classics. London: Penguin, 2003.
———. *The City of God Against the Pagans.* Translated by R. W. Dyson. Cambridge: Cambridge University Press, 1998.
———. *Confessions.* Translated by Henry Chadwick. Oxford: Oxford University Press, 1991.
———. *The Enchiridion on Faith, Hope, and Love.* Edited and translated by Bruce Harbert. Hyde Park, NY: New City, 1999.
———. *On Christian Doctrine.* Translated by D. W. Robertson. New York: Macmillan, 1958.
———. *On Free Choice of the Will.* Translated by Thomas Williams. Indianapolis: Hackett, 1993.
Ayer, Alfred Jules. *Language, Truth and Logic.* New York: Dover, 1952.
Bacchiocchi, Samuele. *Divine Rest for Human Restlessness: A Theological Study of the Good News of the Sabbath for Today.* Berrien Springs: Biblical Perspectives, 1980.
———. *From Sabbath to Sunday: A Historical Investigation of the Rise of Sunday Observance in Early Christianity.* Rome: Pontifical Gregorian University Press, 1977.
Bainton, Roland H. *Here I Stand: A Life of Martin Luther.* New York: Abingdon-Cokesbury, 1950.
———. *The Reformation of the Sixteenth Century.* Boston: Beacon, 1952.
Barth, Karl. *Church Dogmatics.* 1/1: *The Doctrine of the Word of God.* Translated by G. W. Bromiley. Edinburgh: T&T Clark, 1975.
———. *Church Dogmatics.* 1/2: *The Doctrine of the Word of God.* Translated by G. W. Bromiley. Edinburgh: T&T Clark, 1956.

BIBLIOGRAPHY

———. *Church Dogmatics*. 2/1: *The Doctrine of God*. Translated by G. W. Bromiley and T. F. Torrance. Edinburgh: T&T Clark, 1957.
———. *Church Dogmatics*. 2/2: *The Doctrine of God*. Translated by G. W. Bromiley. Edinburgh: T&T Clark, 1957.
———. *Church Dogmatics*. 3/1: *The Doctrine of Creation*. Translated by G. W. Bromiley, J. W. Edwards, O. Bussey, and Harold Knight. Edinburgh: T&T Clark, 1958.
———. *Church Dogmatics*. 3/3: *The Doctrine of Creation*. Translated by G. W. Bromiley and R. J. Ehrlich. Edinburgh: T&T Clark, 1960.
———. *Church Dogmatics*. 4/1: *The Doctrine of Reconciliation*. Translated by G. W. Bromiley. Edinburgh: T&T Clark, 1956.
———. *Church Dogmatics*. 4/2: *The Doctrine of Reconciliation*. Translated by G. W. Bromiley. Edinburgh: T&T Clark, 1958.
———. *Church Dogmatics*. 4/3.1: *The Doctrine of Reconciliation*. Translated by G. W. Bromiley and T. F. Torrance. Edinburgh: T&T Clark, 1961.
Bartholomew, Craig G. *Introducing Biblical Hermeneutics: A Comprehensive Framework for Hearing God in Scripture*. Grand Rapids: Baker Academic, 2015.
Barton, John, and John Muddiman, eds. *The Oxford Bible Commentary*. Oxford: Oxford University Press, 2001.
Bass, Diana Butler. *Freeing Jesus: Rediscovering Jesus as Friend, Teacher, Savior, Lord, Way, and Presence*. New York: HarperOne, 2021.
Batterson, Mark. *Soulprint: Discovering Your Divine Destiny*. Colorado Springs: Multnomah, 2011.
Bauckham, Richard. *The Theology of the Book of Revelation*. Cambridge: Cambridge University Press, 1993.
Bauer, Walter. *A Greek-English Lexicon of the New Testament and Other Early Christian Literature*. 3rd ed. Revised and edited by Frederick W. Danker. Chicago: University of Chicago Press, 2000.
Bauman, Zygmunt. *Liquid Love: On the Frailty of Human Bonds*. Cambridge: Polity, 2003.
Beale, G. K. *The Book of Revelation: A Commentary on the Greek Text*. New International Greek Testament Commentary. Grand Rapids: Eerdmans, 1999.
Berger, Peter L., and Thomas Luckmann. *The Social Construction of Reality: A Treatise in the Sociology of Knowledge*. Garden City, NY: Anchor, 1966.
Berkouwer, G. C. *Sin*. Translated by Philip C. Holtrop. Grand Rapids: Eerdmans, 1971.
Blomberg, Craig L. *1 Corinthians*. Zondervan Exegetical Commentary on the New Testament. Grand Rapids: Zondervan, 2010.
———. *Matthew*. New American Commentary 22. Nashville: Broadman & Holman, 1992.
———. *Neither Poverty Nor Riches: A Biblical Theology of Possessions*. Downers Grove, IL: IVP Academic, 2000.
Bock, Darrell L. *Acts*. Baker Exegetical Commentary on the New Testament. Grand Rapids: Baker Academic, 2007.
Bonhoeffer, Dietrich. *The Cost of Discipleship*. Translated by R. H. Fuller. New York: Macmillan, 1963.
———. *Ethics*. Edited by Clifford J. Green. Translated by Reinhard Krauss et al. Vol. 6 of *Dietrich Bonhoeffer Works*, edited by Wayne Whitson Floyd, Jr. Minneapolis: Fortress, 2005.
———. *Letters and Papers from Prison*. Edited by Eberhard Bethge. New York: Macmillan, 1971.
———. *Life Together*. Translated by John W. Doberstein. New York: HarperOne, 1954.

Braun, Josephine A. "Towards a Contextual Theology of Community: An Exploration of the Body of Christ Metaphor." Masters thesis, McMaster Divinity College, 2010. MacSphere. https://macsphere.mcmaster.ca/handle/11375/10295.

Brown, Francis, et al. *A Hebrew and English Lexicon of the Old Testament*. Oxford: Clarendon, 1906.

Brown, Raymond E. *The Gospel According to John XIII–XXI*. Anchor Bible 29A. Garden City: Doubleday, 1970.

Bruce, F. F. *The Book of the Acts*. New International Commentary on the New Testament. Grand Rapids: Eerdmans, 1988.

———. *The Books and the Parchments: Some Chapters on the Transmission of the Bible*. London: Pickering & Inglis, 1950.

———. *The Canon of Scripture*. Downers Grove, IL: InterVarsity, 1988.

———. *The Epistle to the Hebrews*. New International Commentary on the New Testament. Grand Rapids: Eerdmans, 1990.

———. *Paul: Apostle of the Heart Set Free*. Grand Rapids: Eerdmans, 1977.

Brueggemann, Walter. *Sabbath as Resistance: Saying No to the Culture of Now*. Louisville: Westminster John Knox, 2014.

Bruner, Frederick Dale. *Matthew: A Commentary*. Vol. 1, *The Christbook: Matthew 1–12*. Grand Rapids: Eerdmans, 2007.

Brunner, Emil. *The Christian Doctrine of God*. Translated by Olive Wyon. Philadelphia: Westminster, 1950.

Brunt, John. "Unclean or Unhealthful? An Adventist Perspective." *Spectrum* 11.3 (1981) 17–23.

Bultmann, Rudolf. *Theology of the New Testament*. Translated by Kendrick Grobel. Waco: Baylor University Press, 2007.

Burgess, Glenn. *The Politics of the Ancient Constitution: An Introduction to English Political Thought, 1603–1642*. University Park, PA: Pennsylvania State University Press, 1993.

Busenitz, Irvin A. "Woman's Desire for Man: Genesis 3:16 Reconsidered." *Grace Theological Journal* 7.2 (1986) 203–12.

Butler, Judith. *Gender Trouble: Feminism and the Subversion of Identity*. New York: Routledge, 1990.

Calvin, John. *Institutes of the Christian Religion*. Edited by John T. McNeill. Translated by Ford Lewis Battles. Library of Christian Classics. Philadelphia: Westminster John Knox, 1960.

Campbell, Douglas A. *The Deliverance of God: An Apocalyptic Rereading of Justification in Paul*. Grand Rapids: Eerdmans, 2009.

Carson, D. A. *Showing the Spirit: A Theological Exposition of 1 Corinthians 12–14*. Grand Rapids: Baker Academic, 1987.

Ciampa, Roy E., and Brian S. Rosner. *The First Letter to the Corinthians*. Pillar New Testament Commentary. Grand Rapids: Eerdmans, 2010.

Clement of Rome. *1 Clement*. In *The Apostolic Fathers: Greek Texts and English Translations*, edited and translated by Michael W. Holmes, 12–56. Grand Rapids: Baker Academic, 2007.

Collins, Francis S. *The Language of God: A Scientist Presents Evidence for Belief*. New York: Free Press, 2006.

Cone, James H. *The Cross and the Lynching Tree*. Maryknoll, NY: Orbis, 2011.

———. *God of the Oppressed*. Maryknoll, NY: Orbis, 1997.

BIBLIOGRAPHY

Craigie, Peter C. *The Book of Deuteronomy*. New International Commentary on the Old Testament. Grand Rapids: Eerdmans, 1976.

Creswell, John W. *Research Design: Qualitative, Quantitative, and Mixed Methods Approaches*. 4th ed. Thousand Oaks, CA: Sage, 2014.

Cullmann, Oscar. *Immortality of the Soul or Resurrection of the Dead?* New York: Macmillan, 1958.

Cyprian. "On the Unity of the Catholic Church." In *The Ante-Nicene Fathers: Translations of the Writings of the Fathers down to A.D. 325*, edited by Alexander Roberts and James Donaldson, 5:421–29. Peabody, MA: Hendrickson, 1994.

Daniell, David. *William Tyndale: A Biography*. New Haven, CT: Yale University Press, 1994.

Davidson, Richard M. *A Love of God and Neighbor: The Sabbath and the Character of God*. Berrien Springs, MI: Andrews University Press, 2000.

Davis, David Brion. *The Problem of Slavery in the Age of Revolution, 1770–1823*. Ithaca, NY: Cornell University Press, 1975.

Dawkins, Richard. *The God Delusion*. Boston: Houghton Mifflin, 2006.

Dewey, Arthur J., et al. *The Authentic Letters of Paul: A New Reading of Paul's Rhetoric and Meaning*. Salem: Polebridge, 2010.

Didache. Translated by Michael W. Holmes. In *The Apostolic Fathers: Greek Texts and English Translations*, edited by Michael W. Holmes, 334–55. Grand Rapids: Baker Academic, 2007.

Douglas, Kelly Brown. *Stand Your Ground: Black Bodies and the Justice of God*. Maryknoll, NY: Orbis, 2015.

Douglass, Herbert E. *Messenger of the Lord*. Nampa, ID: Pacific, 1998.

Dunn, James D. G. *Unity and Diversity in the New Testament: An Inquiry into the Character of Earliest Christianity*. 3rd ed. London: SCM, 2006.

Ehrman, Bart D. *Misquoting Jesus: The Story Behind Who Changed the Bible and Why*. New York: HarperCollins, 2005.

Elmer, Ian J. *Paul, Jerusalem and the Judaisers: The Galatian Crisis in Its Broadest Historical Context*. Tübingen: Mohr Siebeck, 2009.

Erickson, Millard J. *Christian Theology*. 2nd ed. Grand Rapids: Baker Academic, 1998.

Eusebius. *The Church History: A New Translation with Commentary*. Translated by Paul L. Maier. Grand Rapids: Kregel, 1999.

Fee, Gordon D. *The First and Second Letters to the Thessalonians*. Grand Rapids: Eerdmans, 2009.

———. *The First Epistle to the Corinthians*. Rev. ed. New International Commentary on the New Testament. Grand Rapids: Eerdmans, 2014.

———. *God's Empowering Presence: The Holy Spirit in the Letters of Paul*. Peabody, MA: Hendrickson, 1994.

———. *Paul, the Spirit, and the People of God*. Peabody, MA: Hendrickson, 1996.

Fee, Gordon D., and Douglas Stuart. *How to Read the Bible for All Its Worth*. 4th ed. Grand Rapids: Zondervan, 2014.

Ferguson, Sinclair B. *The Holy Spirit*. Downers Grove, IL: InterVarsity, 1996.

Finkelstein, Louis, ed. *Sifra on Leviticus*. 5 vols. New York: Jewish Theological Seminary, 1983.

Finley, Mark. *The Last Generation of the Last Days*. Nampa, ID: Pacific, 2022.

Fiorenza, Elisabeth Schüssler. *In Memory of Her: A Feminist Theological Reconstruction of Christian Origins*. New York: Crossroad, 1983.

Fisher, Helen. *Why We Love: The Nature and Chemistry of Romantic Love.* New York: Henry Holt, 2004.
Foucault, Michel. *The History of Sexuality, Volume 1: An Introduction.* Translated by Robert Hurley. New York: Pantheon, 1978.
Forshall, Josiah, and Frederic Madden, eds. *The Holy Bible, Containing the Old and New Testaments, with the Apocryphal Books, in the Earliest English Versions Made from the Latin Vulgate by John Wycliffe and His Followers.* 4 vols. Oxford: Oxford University Press, 1850.
Frame, John M. *The Doctrine of God.* Phillipsburg, NJ: P&R, 2002.
Garland, David E. *1 Corinthians.* Baker Exegetical Commentary on the New Testament. Grand Rapids: Baker Academic, 2003.
———. *2 Corinthians.* New American Commentary 29. Nashville: Broadman & Holman, 1999.
General Conference on Seventh-Day Adventists. *Seventh-day Adventists Believe: An Exposition of the Fundamental Beliefs of the Seventh-day Adventist Church.* 2nd ed. Boise: Pacific, 2005.
Goldingay, John. *Psalms.* Vol. 3, *Psalms 90–150.* Baker Commentary on the Old Testament Wisdom and Psalms. Grand Rapids: Baker Academic, 2008.
González, Justo L. *The Story of Christianity.* Vol. 1, *The Early Church to the Dawn of the Reformation.* New York: HarperOne, 2010.
The Greek New Testament. 5th ed. Stuttgart: Deutsche Bibelgesellschaft, 2014.
Gregory of Nazianzus. *Theological Orations.* In *On God and Christ: The Five Theological Orations and Two Letters to Cledonius,* translated by Frederick Williams and Lionel Wickham, 27–108. Crestwood, NY: St Vladimir's Seminary Press, 2002.
Gregory of Nyssa. *The Great Catechism.* In vol. 5 of *The Nicene and Post-Nicene Fathers,* Series 2, 471–509. Edited by Philip Schaff and Henry Wace. 14 vols. Peabody, MA: Hendrickson, 1994.
———. *On the Soul and the Resurrection.* In vol. 5 of *The Nicene and Post-Nicene Fathers,* Series 2, 429–67. Edited by Philip Schaff and Henry Wace. 14 vols. Peabody, MA: Hendrickson, 1994.
Grenz, Stanley J. *The Moral Quest: Foundations of Christian Ethics.* Downers Grove, IL: InterVarsity, 1997.
Grudem, Wayne. *Evangelical Feminism and Biblical Truth: An Analysis of More Than 100 Disputed Questions.* Wheaton, IL: Crossway, 2004.
———. *Systematic Theology: An Introduction to Biblical Doctrine.* Grand Rapids: Zondervan, 1994.
Gutiérrez, Gustavo. *A Theology of Liberation: History, Politics, and Salvation.* Rev. ed. Maryknoll, NY: Orbis, 1988.
Haddad, Mimi. "Egalitarianism and the New Creation." *Priscilla Papers* 34.2 (2020) 3–9.
Hanegraaff, Hank. *Christianity in Crisis: 21st Century.* Nashville: Thomas Nelson, 2009.
Harrington, Daniel J. "Romans." In *The New Jerome Biblical Commentary,* edited by Raymond E. Brown et al., 853–66. Englewood Cliffs, NJ: Prentice-Hall, 1990.
Harris, Sam. *The End of Faith: Religion, Terror, and the Future of Reason.* New York: Norton, 2004.
Hauerwas, Stanley. *After Christendom? How the Church Is to Behave If Freedom, Justice, and a Christian Nation Are Bad Ideas.* Nashville: Abingdon, 1991.
———. *A Community of Character.* Notre Dame: University of Notre Dame Press, 1981.

BIBLIOGRAPHY

Hays, Richard B. *First Corinthians*. Interpretation: A Bible Commentary for Teaching and Preaching. Louisville: Westminster John Knox, 1997.

———. *The Moral Vision of the New Testament: Community, Cross, New Creation*. San Francisco: HarperOne, 1996.

Heschel, Abraham Joshua. *The Sabbath: Its Meaning for Modern Man*. New York: Farrar, Straus and Giroux, 1951.

Hill, Andrew E. *Malachi: A New Translation with Introduction and Commentary*. Anchor Bible 25D. New York: Doubleday, 1998.

Hoekema, Anthony A. *The Four Major Cults*. Grand Rapids: Eerdmans, 1963.

Holweck, Frederick G. "Church (Etymology of the Word)." In *The Catholic Encyclopedia*, edited by Charles G. Herbermann, 3:744–45. New York: Robert Appleton, 1908.

hooks, bell. *All About Love: New Visions*. New York: William Morrow, 2000.

Hume, David. *Dialogues Concerning Natural Religion*. London: Penguin Classics, 1990.

———. *An Enquiry Concerning Human Understanding*. Edited by Tom L. Beauchamp. Oxford: Oxford University Press, 1999.

Huxley, Thomas H. *Collected Essays*. Vol. 5, *Science and Christian Tradition: Essays*. London: Macmillan, 1894.

Ignatius of Antioch. *Letter to the Ephesians*. In *The Apostolic Fathers*, translated by Bart D. Ehrman, 217–39. Cambridge, MA: Harvard University Press, 2003.

———. *Letter to the Magnesians*. In *The Apostolic Fathers*, translated by Bart D. Ehrman, 241–55. Cambridge, MA: Harvard University Press, 2003.

———. *Letter to the Trallians*. In *The Apostolic Fathers*, translated by Bart D. Ehrman, 257–71. Cambridge, MA: Harvard University Press, 2003.

Illouz, Eva. *Cold Intimacies: The Making of Emotional Capitalism*. Cambridge: Polity, 2007.

Instone-Brewer, David. *Divorce and Remarriage in the Bible: The Social and Literary Context*. Grand Rapids: Eerdmans, 2002.

———. *Divorce and Remarriage in the Church: Biblical Solutions for Pastoral Realities*. Downers Grove, IL: InterVarsity, 2003.

Irenaeus. *Against Heresies*. In *The Ante-Nicene Fathers: Translations of the Writings of the Fathers down to A.D. 325*, edited by Alexander Roberts and James Donaldson, 1:309–567. Peabody, MA: Hendrickson, 1994.

James I. *The True Law of Free Monarchies: Or, The Reciprocal and Mutual Duty Betwixt a Free King and His Natural Subjects*. 1598. In *The Political Works of James I*, edited by Charles Howard McIlwain. Cambridge, MA: Harvard University Press, 1918.

Janssen, Luke J. "The Human Soul: Immaterial Substance or Emergent Property of the Brain?" Presentation at the American Scientific Affiliation Annual Meeting, July 2021.

———. *Soul-Searching: The Evolution of Judeo-Christian Thinking on the Soul and the Afterlife*. Eugene, OR: Wipf & Stock, 2020.

Jefferson, Thomas. *The Declaration of Independence*. 1776. In vol. 1 of *The Papers of Thomas Jefferson*, edited by Julian P. Boyd, 423–32. Princeton: Princeton University Press, 1950.

Jewett, Robert. *Romans: A Commentary*. Minneapolis: Fortress, 2007.

Jones, Timothy Paul. "'Many Parts Yet One Body': How Paul Subverted a Familiar Metaphor." *The Apologetics Newsletter*. Substack, Sept. 3, 2024. https://timothypauljones.substack.com/p/many-parts-yet-one-body-how-pauls.

Kaiser, Walter C., Jr. *Toward an Old Testament Theology*. Grand Rapids: Zondervan, 1978.

———. *Toward Old Testament Ethics*. Grand Rapids: Zondervan, 1983.

Kant, Immanuel. *Critique of Pure Reason.* Translated by Norman Kemp Smith. New York: St. Martin's, 1965.
Käsemann, Ernst. *Commentary on Romans.* Translated by Geoffrey W. Bromiley. Grand Rapids: Eerdmans, 1980.
———. "Principles of the Interpretation of Romans 13." In *New Testament Questions of Today*, 196–216. Philadelphia: Fortress, 1969.
Keener, Craig S. *1-2 Corinthians.* New Cambridge Bible Commentary. Cambridge: Cambridge University Press, 2005.
———. *Acts: An Exegetical Commentary.* Vol. 1. Grand Rapids: Baker Academic, 2012.
———. *Gift and Giver: The Holy Spirit for Today.* Grand Rapids: Baker Academic, 2001.
———. *Paul, Women, and Wives: Marriage and Women's Ministry in the Letters of Paul.* Peabody, MA: Hendrickson, 1992.
———. *Revelation.* NIV Application Commentary. Grand Rapids: Zondervan, 2000.
Keller, Timothy, and Kathy Keller. *The Meaning of Marriage: Facing the Complexities of Commitment with the Wisdom of God.* New York: Riverhead, 2011.
Kierkegaard, Søren. *Fear and Trembling.* Translated by Walter Lowrie. Princeton: Princeton University Press, 1941.
Kipnis, Laura. *Against Love: A Polemic.* New York: Pantheon, 2003.
Kittel, Gerhard, and Gerhard Friedrich, eds. *Theological Dictionary of the New Testament.* Translated by Geoffrey W. Bromiley. 10 vols. Grand Rapids: Eerdmans, 1964–1976.
Klawans, Jonathan. *Impurity and Sin in Ancient Judaism.* New York: Oxford University Press, 2000.
Knight, George R. *Ellen White's World.* Hagerstown, MD: Review and Herald, 1998.
———. *Reading Ellen White.* Hagerstown, MD: Review and Herald, 1997.
Küng, Hans. *The Church.* New York: Sheed and Ward, 1967.
Kuyper, Abraham. *Lectures on Calvinism.* Grand Rapids: Eerdmans, 1931.
Levenson, Jon D. *Creation and the Persistence of Evil: The Jewish Drama of Divine Omnipotence.* Princeton: Princeton University Press, 1988.
Lewis, C. S. *The Four Loves.* New York: Harcourt, 1960.
Liddell, Henry George, and Robert Scott. *A Greek-English Lexicon.* 9th ed. Oxford: Clarendon, 1996.
Locke, John. *An Essay Concerning Human Understanding.* Edited by Peter H. Nidditch. Oxford: Clarendon, 1975.
Longenecker, Richard N. *Acts.* Expositor's Bible Commentary 9. Grand Rapids: Zondervan, 1981.
Luhmann, Niklas. *Love as Passion: The Codification of Intimacy.* Translated by Jeremy Gaines and Doris L. Jones. Stanford: Stanford University Press, 1998.
Luther, Martin. "The Babylonian Captivity of the Church." In *Martin Luther: Selections from His Writings*, edited by John Dillenberger, 11–126. New York: Anchor, 1962.
———. *The Bondage of the Will.* Translated by J. I. Packer and O. R. Johnston. Grand Rapids: Baker Academic, 1957.
———. "The Freedom of a Christian." In *Luther's Works*, vol. 31, *Career of the Reformer I*, edited by Harold J. Grimm, 333–77. Philadelphia: Fortress, 1957.
———. *On Christian Liberty.* Translated by W. A. Lambert. Edited by Harold J. Grimm. Minneapolis: Fortress, 2003.
Luz, Ulrich. *Matthew 8–20.* Hermeneia. Minneapolis: Fortress, 2001.
Maimonides, Moses. *Mishneh Torah: Laws of Forbidden Foods.* Translated by Eliyahu Touger. 20 vols. New York: Moznaim Publishing, 1986–2007.

BIBLIOGRAPHY

Martin, Walter. *The Kingdom of the Cults*. Rev. ed. Minneapolis: Bethany House, 2003.

McDonald, Lee Martin. *The Biblical Canon: Its Origin, Transmission, and Authority*. Peabody, MA: Hendrickson, 2007.

McGrath, Alister E. *The Open Secret: A New Vision for Natural Theology*. Malden, MA: Blackwell, 2008.

———. *A Scientific Theology: Volume 2, Reality*. Grand Rapids: Eerdmans, 2002.

Merriam-Webster. "Complementary." https://www.merriam-webster.com/dictionary/complementary.

Milgrom, Jacob. *Leviticus 1–16*. Anchor Yale Bible Commentary. New Haven, CT: Yale University Press, 1991.

———. *Leviticus 17–22*. Anchor Yale Bible Commentary. New Haven, CT: Yale University Press, 2000.

Moltmann, Jürgen. *The Church in the Power of the Spirit*. Minneapolis: Fortress, 1993.

———. *The Coming of God: Christian Eschatology*. Translated by Margaret Kohl. Minneapolis: Fortress, 1996.

———. *The Crucified God*. Minneapolis: Fortress, 1993.

———. *Theology of Hope*. Translated by James W. Leitch. London: SCM, 1967.

Morris, Leon. *The Gospel According to John*. New International Commentary on the New Testament. Grand Rapids: Eerdmans, 1995.

Mowczko, Marg. *Beyond Authority and Submission*. Eugene, OR: Wipf & Stock, 2019.

Murphy, Nancey, and Joel B. Green. *Whatever Happened to the Soul?* Minneapolis: Fortress, 1998.

Newbigin, Lesslie. *The Gospel in a Pluralist Society*. Grand Rapids: Eerdmans, 1989.

Nygren, Anders. *Commentary on Romans*. Philadelphia: Fortress, 1949.

Oswalt, John N. *The Book of Isaiah, Chapters 40–66*. New International Commentary on the Old Testament. Grand Rapids: Eerdmans, 1998.

Owen, John. *The Works of John Owen*. Vol. 10. Edinburgh: Banner of Truth, 1850.

Packer, J. I. *Knowing God*. Downers Grove, IL: InterVarsity, 1973.

Paxton, Geoffrey J. *The Shaking of Adventism*. Grand Rapids: Baker Book House, 1977.

Pelikan, Jaroslav. *The Christian Tradition: A History of the Development of Doctrine*. Vol. 1, *The Emergence of the Catholic Tradition (100–600)*. Chicago: University of Chicago Press, 1971.

Pierce, Ronald. *Discovering Biblical Equality*. Downers Grove, IL: IVP Academic, 2005.

Piper, John. *This Momentary Marriage: A Parable of Permanence*. Wheaton, IL: Crossway, 2009.

———. *What's the Difference? Manhood and Womanhood Defined According to the Bible*. Wheaton, IL: Crossway, 1990.

Piper, John, and Wayne Grudem, eds. *Recovering Biblical Manhood and Womanhood: A Response to Evangelical Feminism*. Wheaton, IL: Crossway, 2006.

Plantinga, Alvin. *Warranted Christian Belief*. Oxford: Oxford University Press, 2000.

Plantinga, Cornelius, Jr. *Not the Way It's Supposed to Be: A Breviary of Sin*. Grand Rapids: Eerdmans, 1995.

Plato. *Phaedo*. Translated by G. M. A. Grube. Indianapolis: Hackett, 1977.

Polkinghorne, John. *The Faith of a Physicist: Reflections of a Bottom-Up Thinker*. Princeton: Princeton University Press, 1994.

———. *The God of Hope and the End of the World*. New Haven, CT: Yale University Press, 2002.

Polanyi, Michael. *Personal Knowledge: Towards a Post-Critical Philosophy.* Chicago: University of Chicago Press, 1958.
Popper, Karl. *Conjectures and Refutations: The Growth of Scientific Knowledge.* London: Routledge, 2002.
———. *The Logic of Scientific Discovery.* London: Routledge, 1959.
Rashi. *Commentary on Leviticus.* Brooklyn: Soncino, 1982.
Ratzlaff, Dale. *The Cultic Doctrine of Seventh-Day Adventists.* Glendale: Life Assurance Ministries, 1996.
Russell, Bertrand. *Why I Am Not a Christian.* London: Routledge, 1957.
Schiel, Katy. *Monarchy: A Primary Source Analysis.* New York: Rosen, 2004.
Schnackenburg, Rudolf. *The Gospel According to St. John.* Vol. 3. Translated by David Smith and G. A. Kon. New York: Crossroad, 1982.
Schreiner, Thomas R. *The Law and Its Fulfillment: A Pauline Theology of Law.* Grand Rapids: Baker Academic, 1993.
Septuaginta: With Morphology. Rev. ed. Edited by Alfred Rahlfs and Robert Hanhart. Stuttgart: Deutsche Bibelgesellschaft, 2006.
Smith, James K. A. *Desiring the Kingdom: Worship, Worldview, and Cultural Formation.* Grand Rapids: Baker Academic, 2009.
Spinoza, Baruch. *Tractatus Theologico-Politicus.* Translated by Samuel Shirley. Leiden: Brill, 1991.
Sproul, R. C. *The Holiness of God.* 2nd ed. Wheaton, IL: Tyndale House, 1998.
Stern, David H. *Restoring the Jewishness of the Gospel.* Clarksville, MD: Jewish New Testament Publications, 1988.
Stott, John R. W. *Issues Facing Christians Today.* London: Marshall Pickering, 1984.
Stuart, Douglas. *Hosea–Jonah.* Word Biblical Commentary 31. Dallas: Word, 1987.
Stump, Eleonore. *Wandering in Darkness: Narrative and the Problem of Suffering.* Oxford: Oxford University Press, 2010.
Swinburne, Richard. *Are We Bodies or Souls?* Oxford: Oxford University Press, 2019.
———. *The Evolution of the Soul.* Rev. ed. Oxford: Clarendon, 1997.
Taylor, Charles. *Sources of the Self: The Making of the Modern Identity.* Cambridge, MA: Harvard University Press, 1989.
Tertullian. *De Anima.* In *The Ante-Nicene Fathers: Translations of the Writings of the Fathers down to A.D. 325,* edited by Alexander Roberts and James Donaldson, 3:181–235. Peabody, MA: Hendrickson, 1994.
Thiselton, Anthony C. *The First Epistle to the Corinthians.* New International Greek Testament Commentary. Grand Rapids: Eerdmans, 2000.
Thompson, Alden. *Escape from the Flames: How Ellen White Grew from Fear to Joy—and Helped Me Do It Too.* Nampa, ID: Pacific, 2003.
Tillich, Paul. *The Courage to Be.* New Haven, CT: Yale University Press, 1952.
———. *Dynamics of Faith.* New York: Harper & Row, 1957.
———. *Systematic Theology.* Vol. 3. Chicago: University of Chicago Press, 1963.
Timm, Alberto R. "The Spirit of Prophecy in the Advent Movement." In *The Ellen G. White Encyclopedia,* edited by Denis Fortin and Jerry Moon, 1245–48. Hagerstown, MD: Review and Herald, 2013.
Tonstad, Sigve K. *The Lost Meaning of the Seventh Day.* Berrien Springs, MI: Andrews University Press, 2009.
Torrance, T. F. *The Trinitarian Faith: The Evangelical Theology of the Ancient Catholic Church.* Edinburgh: T&T Clark, 1988.

Trible, Phyllis. *God and the Rhetoric of Sexuality*. Philadelphia: Fortress, 1978.
Trueman, Carl R. *The Rise and Triumph of the Modern Self: Cultural Amnesia, Expressive Individualism, and the Road to Sexual Revolution*. Wheaton, IL: Crossway, 2020.
Twenge, Jean M. *iGen: Why Today's Super-Connected Kids Are Growing Up Less Rebellious, More Tolerant, Less Happy—and Completely Unprepared for Adulthood*. New York: Atria, 2017.
Tyndale, William. *The New Testament*. Antwerp: Merten de Keyser, 1526. British Library. https://www.bl.uk/collection-items/william-tyndales-new-testament.
Tyndale, William, trans. *The New Testament: A Facsimile of the 1526 Edition*. Edited by W. R. Cooper. London: British Library, 2000.
Van Inwagen, Peter. "The Possibility of Resurrection." In *Philosophy and the Christian Faith*, edited by Thomas V. Morris, 119–40. Notre Dame: University of Notre Dame Press, 1988.
Van Til, Cornelius. *The Defense of the Faith*. 4th ed. Phillipsburg, NJ: P&R, 2008.
Vanhoozer, Kevin J. *The Drama of Doctrine: A Canonical-Linguistic Approach to Christian Theology*. Louisville: Westminster John Knox, 2005.
Von Balthasar, Hans Urs. *Theo-Drama: Theological Dramatic Theory*. Vol. 5, *The Last Act*. San Francisco: Ignatius, 1998.
Walton, John H. *Genesis*. NIV Application Commentary. Grand Rapids: Zondervan, 2001.
———. *The Lost World of Genesis One: Ancient Cosmology and the Origins Debate*. Downers Grove, IL: InterVarsity, 2009.
Watts, John D. W. *Joel, Obadiah, Jonah, Nahum, Habakkuk, and Zephaniah*. Cambridge Bible Commentary. Cambridge: Cambridge University Press, 1975.
Webster, John. *Holy Scripture: A Dogmatic Sketch*. Cambridge: Cambridge University Press, 2003.
Wenham, Gordon J. *The Book of Leviticus*. New International Commentary on the Old Testament. Grand Rapids: Eerdmans, 1979.
———. *Exploring the Old Testament: A Guide to the Pentateuch*. Downers Grove, IL: InterVarsity, 2003.
———. *Genesis 1–15*. Word Biblical Commentary 1. Dallas: Word, 1987.
———. *Story as Torah: Reading Old Testament Narrative Ethically*. Grand Rapids: Baker Academic, 2000.
Whidden, Woodrow W. *Ellen White on Salvation*. Hagerstown, MD: Review and Herald, 1995.
White, Ellen G. *Counsels on Diet and Foods*. Washington, DC: Review and Herald, 1938.
———. *The Desire of Ages*. Mountain View: Pacific, 1898.
———. *Early Writings*. Hagerstown, MD: Review and Herald, 1882.
White, James. "Swine's Flesh." *Present Truth* 1.10 (1872) 87.
Witherington, Ben, III. *Women in the Earliest Churches*. Cambridge: Cambridge University Press, 1988.
Wittgenstein, Ludwig. *On Certainty*. Translated by Denis Paul and G. E. M. Anscombe. Oxford: Basil Blackwell, 1969.
Wood, Gordon S. *The Creation of the American Republic, 1776–1787*. Chapel Hill, NC: University of North Carolina Press, 1969.
Wright, N. T. *The Case for the Psalms: Why They Are Essential*. New York: HarperOne, 2014.
———. *Jesus and the Victory of God*. Minneapolis: Fortress, 1996.
———. *Matthew for Everyone, Part 1*. Louisville: Westminster John Knox, 2004.
———. *Matthew for Everyone, Part 2*. Louisville: Westminster John Knox, 2004.

———. *The New Testament and the People of God*. Minneapolis: Fortress, 1992.

———. *Paul: A Biography*. San Francisco: HarperOne, 2018.

———. *Paul and the Faithfulness of God*. Christian Origins and the Question of God 4. Minneapolis: Fortress, 2013.

———. *The Resurrection of the Son of God*. Minneapolis: Fortress, 2003.

———. *Surprised by Hope: Rethinking Heaven, the Resurrection, and the Mission of the Church*. New York: HarperOne, 2008.

Wycliffe, John, trans. *The Wycliffe Bible (Early Version)*. Circa 1382. MS. Bodl. 277. *Digital Bodleian*. Oxford University. https://digital.bodleian.ox.ac.uk/objects/bfbb83b1-9ee3-49a7-a434-ef0f602d2350/.

General Index

Abuse of Power in Church Systems, xi–xiii, 79
Adam and Eve, 1, 6, 15, 21, 27, 88–89
Adams, Marilyn McCord, 4
Agnosticism, 119–120, 144
Anabaptists, 75
Aquinas, Thomas, 12, 16
Aristotle, 27, 55
Athanasius, 2, 106
Atonement Theories (Substitutionary), 22
Augustine, 2, 3, 10, 11, 15, 20, 26, 39, 48, 74, 79, 113
Authority, Divine, 142–147
Authority, Institutional, xi–xiii, 71–83, 84–85, 148–154

Bacchiocchi, Samuele, 38, 41, 42
Barth, Karl, 16, 26, 45, 50, 69, 75, 114, 120, 144
Bauman, Zygmunt, 28
Beale, G. K., 46, 63
Berger, Peter, 10
Bible, as Word of God, 43–52
Bonhoeffer, Dietrich, 27, 77
Brueggemann, Walter, 42
Brunner, Emil, 45
Bultmann, Rudolf, 45
Burton, Keith A., ix–xi, xix
Butler, Judith, 28

Calvin, John, 11, 16, 74, 114

Carson, D. A., 99, 101
Charismata (χαρίσματα), 96–98, 100
Christian Nationalism, 77
Church, Institutional vs. *Ekklesia*, 71–83; 84–95
Clean/Unclean Distinctions, 136–141
Clement of Rome, 74
Complementarity (Gender), 84–95
Cone, James, 77, 83
Conditional Immortality, 53–61
Covenant Theology, 49–52, 76
Covenant, Marriage and Divorce, 30–37
Crichton, Jerome C., 5, 6, 159
Cullmann, Oscar, 58
Cyprian, 79

Davidson, Richard M., 39, 41
Dawkins, Richard, 119
Divine Hiddenness, 112–125
Divine Love, 19–24; 25–29
Douglass, Herbert E., 66
Douglass, Kelly Brown, 76, 83
Dualism (Platonic/Hellenistic), 53, 57, 59–60

Early Church / Patristics, 2–3, 11, 15–16, 54, 106
Ekklesia (ἐκκλησία), 71–83, 84–95
Empiricism, 20, 113, 118
Enlightenment, 11, 27, 44, 51, 113
Entropy, 104–111

GENERAL INDEX

Epistemology (Faith vs. Reason), 112–125
Erickson, Millard, 16
Eschatology, 5–6, 13, 60, 76, 107–108, 110–111
Evil, Problem of, 1–6; 24

Faith, 112–125
Fee, Gordon D., 34–35, 46, 64, 81, 97–100
Finley, Mark, 65
Fisher, Helen, 28
Forgiveness, 23–24
Foucault, Michel, 27

Gender Roles, 84–95
Glorification, 104–111
Goldingay, John, 49
Gregory of Nazianzus, 11
Gregory of Nyssa, 3, 54, 106
Grenz, Stanley, 29
Grudem, Wayne, 16, 45, 91

Haddad, Mimi, 94
Hanegraaff, Hank, 68
Hauerwas, Stanley, 75
Hays, Richard B., 34, 99, 144
Hermeneutics, ix–xi, xvii
Heschel, Abraham Joshua, 39
Hiddenness of God, 112–125
Hoekema, Anthony A., 67, 68
Holiness, 38–42
hooks, bell, 28
Hume, David, 20, 113, 119

Illouz, Eva, 27
Irenaeus, 1, 6, 16, 54, 61

Janssen, Luke, 59–60
Jerusalem Council, 80–82

Kant, Immanuel, 113
Keener, Craig, 64, 98
Keller, Timothy, 32
Kierkegaard, Søren, 118
Kipnis, Laura, 28
Knight, George R., 66–67

Küng, Hans, 85
Kuyper, Abraham, 10

Liberation, 22–23
Locke, John, 113
Love, Divine vs. Human, 19–24; 25–29
Luckmann, Thomas, 10
Luhmann, Niklas, 27
Luther, Martin, xii, xvi, 11, 16, 27, 74

Marriage and Divorce, 30–37
Materialism, 19–20, 43–45, 112–118
McGrath, Alister, 10, 17, 108
Moltmann, Jürgen, 28, 37, 108
Morris, Leon, 105
Mowczko, Marg, 94
Murphy, Nancey, 55, 60

Natural Law, 12–13
Newbigin, Lesslie, 75
Nygren, Anders, 80

Ordination, Women's, 84–95

Packer, J. I., 26, 45
Paxton, Geoffrey J., 67
Pelagius, 16
Piper, John, 33, 91
Plantinga, Alvin, 12, 21, 113–114, 120
Plantinga, Cornelius, 16
Plato, 54–55, 57
Polanyi, Michael, 117, 119
Polkinghorne, John, 55, 58, 107–108
Postmodernity, 11, 13
Progressive Revelation, Postscript, 155–158; xi–xii

Queer Identified, 148–154

Ratzlaff, Dale, 67
Redemption, 22
Redemptive Immunization Theodicy (RIT), 1–6
Reformation, Protestant, 11, 74
Remnant Theology, 62–70
Restoration, 23

RIT (Redemptive Immunization
    Theodicy), 1–6

Sabbath, 38–42
Sacrifice, 22
Salvation History, 63
Sensus Divinitatis, 114
Sin, Chapter 3, 14–18
Social Construction of Reality, 7–13
Soul, Conditionalist View, 53–61
Soul-Print, 53–61
Spinoza, Baruch, 44
Spirit of Prophecy, 65–68
Spiritual Gifts Fallacy, 96–103
Sproul, R. C., 26
Stump, Eleonore, 3
Swinburne, Richard, 59

Taylor, Charles, 27
Tertullian, 54
Theodicy, 1–6
Theology, as Art and Science, Postscript, 155–158
Thiselton, Anthony C., 34–35, 46, 98
Thompson, Alden, 67

Tillich, Paul, 117
Timm, Alberto R., 66
Tithing, 126–130
Tonstad, Sigve K., 38, 40
Torrance, T. F., 109
Transformation, 23
Trible, Phyllis, 91
Trueman, Carl, 27
Twenge, Jean, 27, 28
Tyndale, William, 86, 97–98, 102

Vanhoozer, Kevin J., 10, 48–49, 50
Van Inwagen, Peter, 55, 58
Van Til, Cornelius, 10
Von Balthasar, Hans Urs, 3

Webster, John, 49
Wenham, Gordon, 31, 37, 49
Whidden, Woodrow W., 66
White, Ellen G., 64–68
Witherington, Ben, III, 35
Women in Ministry, 84–95
Wright, N. T., 32, 45, 50, 55, 60, 81, 83, 97, 108

Scripture Index

OLD TESTAMENT

Genesis

1:1	20
1:3	8
1:26–27	20, 21
1:27	13
1:28	7
1:31	26
2:1–3	39
2:3	39, 42
2:7	54, 55
2:15	21
2:16–17	1, 21
2:17	2, 6
2:18–25	95, 88–89
2:19	7
2:19–20	8
3:1–4	24
3:1–19	15
3:5	2
3:16	89–91, 94, 95
3:17–19	15
3:22	1
4:7	89
4:26	63
7:23	62
8:22	21
9:25	xiv
12:1–3	63
16:4–6	36
29:30–30:24	36
39:9	15

Exodus

20:2, 11	39
20:11	42
24:7	49
29:43	39
34:6–7	26

Leviticus

11	136
19:2	26
21:8	39
23:1–44	41
25:47–55	22

Deuteronomy

4:2	47
18:22	66
24:1	31
24:1–4	31
29	112

1 Samuel

16:13	131

SCRIPTURE INDEX

2 Samuel
11:2–27	36

1 Kings
11:1–8	36
19:18	63

2 Chronicles
7:14	23

Ezra
9:10	23

Job
1–2	15, 17, 18

Psalms
14:1	121
19:1	12
19:1–2	117
19:1, 7	12
19:7	12
23	49
34:18	24
37	63
42:1–2	60
53:1	146
68:18 (LXX)	99, 100
119:11	48, 51
119:89	49, 52
119:105	10, 47
136:1	26
139:16	24
139:16, 23–24	56, 15
146:4	54

Proverbs
3:5	47, 48, 51
18:21	8

Ecclesiastes
12:7	24, 54, 55

Isaiah
1:9	62
1:11–17	79
5:20	9
6:3	26
6:13	62
10:20–23	62
10:22	62
28:11	102
31:3	26
42:21	41
45	112
45:15	112
50:6	22
52:14	22
53	45
53:5, 12	15
59:2	14
64:6	23
65:17	2

Jeremiah
1:2	46
3:6–10	28
3:8	31
17:9	15, 17
31:3	26
31:33	50, 52

Ezekiel
2:4	47
16	35
16:32	31
23	35

Hosea
1:2–3:5	36
2:11	41
2:14–20	28, 30, 37
4:12	31

Joel
2:23	131
2:28–29	88

SCRIPTURE INDEX

Amos

1:3	47

Malachi

2:16	31
3:16	56

NEW TESTAMENT

Matthew

4:18–22	47
5–7	47, 52
5:5	63
5:13–16	71, 73
5:17	41, 47
5:21–28	15, 17
5:21–48	9
5:22	121
5:39–40	142
7:21–23	79
10:28	56, 58
11:29	xxi
11:28–30	40
13:24–30	79
16:18	72, 73, 93
18:21–35	23
18:22	24
19:3–6	32
19:3–9	35
19:8	36
21:1–11	82
23	79
24:31	76
26:12	87

Mark

2:27–28	40
2:28	41
3:14	85
16:1–16	87
16:7, 10, 11, 14	87

Luke

4:16	40, 41
5:18–25	23
5:27–28	47
8:1–3	86
10:26	xiv
19:8–9	23
20:38	54
22:20	50
23:34	23
24:1–12	86

John

1:1	105
1:1–3	7, 8
1:1–14	44
1:14	13, 24, 50, 52
3:6	94
3:16	26
4:7–26	29
4:23–24	76
4:24	114, 116
5:26	105
5:39	xiv
8:7	xv
8:11	29
10:12	79
10:14	72
10:16	82
10:27	71
11:25	57
11:25–26	54
12:3	86
12:27–28	105
12:32	82
12:49–50	46, 47
14:15	26
15:7	49
16:1–4	xii
16:13	xii, 9, 11, 113
17:1–5	107
17:2–3	107
17:4–5	104, 105, 110
17:6–8	104, 109
17:18, 23	109, 110
17:20–24	2, 3, 6
17:21–23	72, 109
17:22–24	106

SCRIPTURE INDEX

John (continued)

17:24	108
20:27	5
20:29	46

Acts

2	75
2:4–11	101
2:16–21	131
2:33	131
2:42	48, 51
2:42–44	114
2:42–47	49
7:38	72
9:1–19	23
10	xv
13:14	41
13:42, 44	41
13:48	85
14:23	85
15	80, 81
15:1–35	80
15:11	69
15:20	136
17:11	xvii
17:22–31	117
17:28	55, 121
19:32	73

Romans

1:18–20	24
1:18–23	119, 144
1:18–32	15
1:19–20	114
1:20	7, 8, 9, 10, 11, 12, 13, 115
1:20–27	13
1:21	114
1:25	27
2:1–3	18
2:4	29
2:14–15	12, 22, 116
3:23	14, 15
5	2
5:8	26
5:8–9	22
5:12	22
5:12–21	15
5:20	2, 18
5:20–21	18
6:5	75
7:7	142
7:12	41
7:18–25	15
8:12–23	131
8:13	18
8:18–21	1
8:18–23	107, 110
8:19–22	15, 17, 18
8:20–21	56
8:28–39	47, 52
8:29–30	105, 106
9:27–29	63
10:4	142
10:12–13	69
10:17	114
11:5	62, 63, 64
11:17–24	63, 64
12:1–2	142
12:2	9, 12, 48, 50, 51
12:3	114, 116, 119, 120, 144
12:4–5	78, 80, 100
13:1–7	142
14:5–6	41
14:14	136

1 Corinthians

2:16	9
5:1–5	35
7:10–11	33
7:10–16	33
7:15	33, 35
12	75, 92, 95, 96
12:1	93, 96, 102
12:1–31	96, 116
12:4	98
12:7	80, 93, 97, 101, 103
12:8–10	97
12:11	103
12:12–13	101
12:12–14	80
12:12–27	64, 72, 78

180

12:12–31	92, 96
12:18	97
12:21–26	101
12:27	69, 75
12:28	66
12:31	80, 82
13:4–7	26
13:6	27
13:12	5
14:1–19	103
14:1–5	103
14:6–9	103
14:10–11	102
14:21–22	102
14:26	103
14:34–35	94
14:37	43, 46, 51
15:26	107
15:42–44	24, 57
15:42–49	105, 106, 107
15:42–54	110
15:53–54	61
15:57	18
15:58	76

2 Corinthians

4:2	97
4:3–4	116
4:16–18	107
5:14	26
5:21	22
10:5	13
11:2	36
12:7–10	xiv

Galatians

1:11–17	82
1:13–16	xv
2:1–10	80
2:9	81
3:14	131
3:28	xiv, 64, 93, 94, 95
4:9–10	41
5:1	22
5:22–23	75, 99, 120
6:1–5	23

Ephesians

1:3–14	75
1:7–8	22
1:22–23	69, 75
2:11–22	64
2:19–22	78
2:20–22	72
2:22	78
4:1–6	72
4:3	72
4:3–6	69
4:4	69
4:5	80
4:7	142
4:7–11	100
4:8	99, 100
4:11	66
4:11–16	78, 100
4:15	29
4:31–32	24
5:21	93
5:21–33	93
5:23	80
5:25	28
5:25–27	36, 72
5:27	26

Philippians

2:6–8	105
2:10–11	24
2:15–16	77
3:20–21	107, 108

Colossians

1:13–18	80, 81
1:15–17	115
1:15–20	13, 115
1:18	75, 80, 82
2:15	15, 17, 18
2:16–17	40, 50
3:4	107
3:11	64

1 Thessalonians

2:13	43, 46, 51

SCRIPTURE INDEX

1 Timothy
2:7	86
2:11–15	94

2 Timothy
2:15	63
2:19	71
3:16	44, 45, 47, 50, 51

Titus
1:5	85, 86
3:4–7	26

Hebrews
1:2	131
1:3	8
1:10–12	56
4:3–11	131
4:9	40, 41
4:9–11	40
4:12	45, 49
5:8–9	107
7:1–3	131
8:10	50
9:15	50
10:1	50, 52
10:24–25	114
11:1	18, 46, 52, 113
11:3	7, 8, 9, 10, 11, 12, 13, 24, 115, 119, 144
11:36–38	76
12:6	26
12:14	131
12:22	50

James
4:17	17
5:16	23

1 Peter
1:15–16	26
2:4–5	78
2:24	22

2 Peter
1:4	105
1:20–21	65
1:21	45, 46
3:13	107
3:16	46, 47

1 John
3:4	14, 15, 17
4:1–3	66
4:8	19, 20, 21, 24, 26
4:10	26
4:12	24
4:16	26

Revelation
1:1–3	43, 46, 51, 68
1:2,	9 68
2–3	73
3:1	79
4:11	20
5:6	3
10:6–7	24
12:17	62, 63, 64, 65, 68, 69, 70
13:8	21
14:12	68
19:7–9	28, 76, 78
19:10	65, 66, 67, 68
20:14–15	58
21:1–5	13
21:2	36, 72, 78
21:3–4	2
21:4	107
21:9	36
22:3–5	23, 24

www.ingramcontent.com/pod-product-compliance
Lightning Source LLC
Chambersburg PA
CBHW072128160426
43197CB00012B/2028